cipal
the
olism

COPING WITH
SUBSTANCE ABUSE

COPING WITH SUBSTANCE ABUSE

RHODA MCFARLAND

THE ROSEN PUBLISHING GROUP, INC.
NEW YORK

Published in 1987, 1990 by The Rosen Publishing Group, Inc.
29 East 21st Street, New York, NY 10010

Copyright 1987, 1990 by Rhoda McFarland

Revised Edition 1990

Library of Congress Cataloging-in-Publication Data

McFarland, Rhoda.
 Coping with substance abuse.

 Includes index.
 1. Youth—United States—Substance use—Prevention.
2. Substance abuse—United States—Prevention. I. Title.
HV4999.Y68M26   1987   362.2′9′088054   87-16537   Index
ISBN 0-8239-1135-7

Manufactured in the United States of America

About the Author

Rhoda McFarland is a teacher who has had experience teaching all grades kindergarten through twelfth grade. At the junior and senior high levels she has taught a variety of academic subjects and has been a band and choir director as well. She is still active as a musician and plays bass clarinet in the Sacramento Valley Symphonic Band, a community organization of nonprofessional musicians.

Ms. McFarland has worked with troubled young people and their parents as a teacher and certified alcoholism and drug abuse counselor. She is responsible for writing and implementing the first educational program in the central California area for students making the transition from drug/alcohol treatment programs back into the regular school system. Because of her extensive training and background in the field of chemical dependency, she is sought as a consultant by treatment facilities, parent groups, and educational programs. She is highly respected in her community for her talents and dedication in helping troubled families.

Introduction

Chemical abuse is all around you; it is part of your everyday world. Much has been written about what drugs and alcohol do to your body, but what do they do to friendships and to families? How do people who are alcoholic or addicted to drugs behave? How do people who use chemicals* feel? How do the people who love and care about chemical abusers behave and feel? What is it like to have a parent who drinks too much, a brother or sister who abuses drugs, a friend who no longer cares for you but would rather get high with new-found friends? What can you do to help people who abuse chemicals?

This book can help you find the answers to those questions and give you new insights into the puzzling disease of chemical dependency. The behavior of chemically dependent people and their families is described and explored. If the descriptions seem to fit people in your life, then take the steps indicated to help them get the help they need; but most of all, do what you need to do to get the help *you* need to cope with living in a world of chemical abusers.

---

*Throughout the book the term "chemical" is used to refer to any and all drugs, including alcohol and prescription drugs.

Contents

COPING WITH
SUBSTANCE ABUSE

CHAPTER I

The Problem

Putting her books on the table and grabbing an apple to munch, Anne Average went in to watch "Once Upon a Lifetime" with her mother. It was their favorite soap opera, and Anne was delighted to see Trudy and Tim talking earnestly over drinks in a dimly lit cocktail lounge. After the commercial for Meltaway, a new diet pill that promised to melt those pounds away with no hunger pangs or your money back, the story continued at the home of Winifred, Trudy's mother. Winifred was talking to her attorney, Marcus, who was at the bar fixing drinks.

Later that evening, Anne's father and brother cheered during the sports report on the news when the game-winning home run sailed over the beer sign on the left field fence and their team won the World Series. After the news, Dad and Anne's brother, Allen, settled down to watch the football game. Anne had told her brother about one beer commercial that she thought was obnoxious because the men were so rough and tough, so Allen was especially anxious to see it. There were three other beer commercials—one saying that beer was the workingman's drink, one with athletes standing at the bar shouting about light beer, and a third showing cowhands enjoying a "cool one" at the end of the day—before the one that Anne disliked came on. Allen defended it, resulting in a few words between him and Anne. Dad told them both to quiet down so he could watch the game.

Mom came in about then to say that she had a miserable headache and was going to take some aspirin and lie down for a while. Allen suggested that she try the latest extra-strength painkiller that was supposed to work faster and longer.

After the game was over, Anne switched to her favorite evening soap opera. She loved to see the women all dressed up when the family had cocktails before dinner. That was the way to live! Allen thought the big-time wheeling and dealing that the men did was great, to say nothing of the beautiful women falling all

1

over them. Those long two-martini lunches that went on into the afternoon were for him.

MESSAGES FROM THE MEDIA

The examples of Anne and Allen Average are not exaggerated. If anything, they show a minimum of what you see and hear every day. You are constantly bombarded with "do drugs" messages. What do you need for a happy relationship? Try a bottle of Velvet Comfort and you will be sexy and appealing to that glamorous lover just waiting for you. Are you overweight and unappealing? All you need is a pill to make you slim and beautiful. Do you have an ache or a pain? Try extra-strength Uforia tablets and you will forget the pain in minutes. Do you want to be charming and attractive? Just use Charmo toothpaste, and you will have more dates than you know what to do with. Do you have the sniffles? No need to put up with the discomfort of a cold. Take Contrail long-acting decongestant, antihistamine, low-sodium, sniffle-inhibiting capsules with the red, yellow, white, and orange beads inside. Are you having trouble attracting that special someone? It must be that you have not tried Tacky Mints, the breath mint that will bring that someone close to you. Having a problem getting along with your friends? Just try Springboard soap, and your problems will be over.

The message is very simple. Everyone should be pain-free, beautiful, and popular. If you are not, there is a pill or a paste or a soap that will fix it for you. Feel good. Physical and emotional pain are unnatural, and you must do something to make the pain go away.

Magazine ads show the gorgeous, sexy woman and the handsome man, their heads close together so they can sniff the brandy in the glass. Want to get together with a beautiful woman or a handsome man? Drink Magnifico brandy. The romanticizing of drinking by the media tells you that you can be better-looking, happier, more popular, and more sophisticated by drinking.

Movies glamorize drinking and make comedies about drunks. Where do the beautiful people go?—to parties where waiters pass champagne on large trays. When you want to have a private conversation with someone, where do you meet?—at an out-of-the-way bar, of course. If our movie hero is having a difficult time, what does he need?—a drink. If our leading lady is going to look sophisticated, she has a cigarette in one hand and a drink in the other. Paul Newman's role as an alcoholic attorney in "The Verdict" earned him an Academy Award nomination. Dudley Moore was a rich, funny drunk in the movie "Arthur," and his demand as an actor went up afterward. Hollywood has done such a good job selling the acceptance of alcohol that alcoholism has become a significant problem in the movie capital.

People getting stoned in movies is everyday stuff. Lily Tomlin, Dolly Parton, and Jane Fonda got stoned in the movie "9 to 5." Cheech and Chong have made a fortune making movies about getting loaded. Their comedy records sell by the thousands, and most of their jokes are drug-oriented.

Songs about getting high and using drugs are common. The songs of many heavy metal rock groups are about drugs. Drug use is so glamorized that when sports stars, movie stars, rock stars, and TV stars are arrested for drug possession, no one is terribly upset, and for some it does not interfere with their career. Stacy Keach did six months in a British jail, and his job as TV's Mike Hammer was waiting for him. Stars overdose and die and become immortal—Janis Joplin, Jimmi Hendrix, John Belushi. They are remembered as wonderful performers, geniuses, and their drug addiction is brushed aside as unimportant or, worse yet, something to be copied.

When Len Bias, who had just been drafted by the Boston Celtics, and Don Rogers of the Cleveland Browns football team died of cocaine poisoning within eight days of each other in June, 1986, the nation was shocked. Both young men were celebrating important events, Bias the reality of his dream of playing basketball for the Celtics and Rogers his coming marriage. They were reportedly not known as drug users, so there was much discussion about whether they were regular users or inept beginners. Was the sports world trying to say that their using cocaine was not as bad if they were not regular users? What difference does it make when they are both dead as a result of the fine American tradition of celebrating an important event by getting high on your drug of choice? What difference does it make where they got the stuff or who gave it to them? Former Cleveland Browns coach Sam Rutigliano said in newspaper reports that he was sure Rogers used as a result of peer pressure, that he was introduced to drugs by teammates and used them so he would be accepted. Since Bias was not known as a user, he probably experienced the same feelings and need for acceptance. It is hard to resist when everybody who is celebrating with you is getting high and feeling wonderful and thinks you are not with it unless you try this great stuff they have to share with you. After all, it makes you feel even better, and it won't hurt you to try it—or will it? What a price to pay to be "one of the guys"!

Bias and Rogers made headlines because they were famous athletes. What about the thousands of unknowns who died of drug overdoses in 1986? Let's not talk about them; let's pretend they did not happen is the general attitude in society. Americans do not want the drug boat rocked because too many are riding on it.

DRUG USE IS ACCEPTED

The most widely used drug in America is alcohol. It is as American as apple pie. Americans drink to anything and everything. Celebrate a birthday with a drink. Drink a toast to the bride and groom and to the new parents when a baby is born. Drink when you are happy and when you are sad. Drink to celebrate winning the game or to mourn losing it. Drink on holidays and on hot summer days or cold winter evenings. Honor the new boss with a drink. Do you need an excuse to drink? You can surely find one for any occasion.

Drinking is considered "something that all teens try." Its seriousness is downplayed. When Son comes home drunk, Dad says, "Boys will be boys; I remember what it's like to be a kid and drink a little booze at a party."

Alcohol use is so accepted in our culture that you are ridiculed and made to feel different if you do not drink. There was even a campaign with the slogan, "It's okay not to drink." In our society it has become necessary to give permission and reassurance that you are okay even if you choose not to drink.

For every ache or pain you can possibly have, the drug companies of America have found a pain reliever. From head to foot there is a pill, liquid, tablet, cream, gel, powder, lotion, paste, lozenge, spray, mist, drop, capsule, or caplet that will make you feel better in a flash. Americans buy drugs over the counters of supermarkets, drugstore chains, neighborhood pharmacies, convenience stores, and a variety of other businesses. From birth on, children are given drugs without a thought that the pattern of taking something to feel better is being encouraged and promoted. If you get home from school and have a headache, does your mother tell you to lie down for a while and see if being quiet helps? Does she ask if you skipped lunch and suggest that the headache may be a result of waiting too long before eating, or does she remind you where the aspirin is kept?

From Meltaway to heroin, everybody's doing it. You can get it at the convenience store on the corner, at the supermarket, at school, or from your dealer down the street. You can even get it from your family physician, sometimes without asking. If the doctor thinks you may suffer some pain with your infected ear, he will write you a prescription for codeine. If you complain about the pain, you can keep getting prescriptions long after the pain is gone. If you have a tooth pulled, the dentist will be happy to give you a prescription for the pain you *might* have. Whatever your drug, legal or illegal, you can find it within a few minutes.

You have received a double message from adults who reach into the medicine chest at the slightest discomfort and then condemn drug use. When you want something to fix every ache or pain, you have accepted the media message that the use of drugs will make your world better. When you laugh at the drunks on TV and in the movies and think they are cool, when you think you have to drink to be accepted, when you believe a drink makes you appear sophisticated, when watching people getting loaded in movies seems ordinary, you have accepted the drug use around you. You have become part of the problem.

PARENTS SIGNAL ACCEPTANCE OF DRUGS

When Larry Licit's dad gets home from his law office every evening, he make himself a stiff Scotch and water and sits down to relax and read the newspaper before dinner. Oscar Ordinary's dad likes to have a beer and watch the news on TV when he gets home from work. In the evening after dinner, Sarah Sixtee's parents like to smoke a joint. The Sixtees began using marijuana when they were in college, and although they do not use alcohol at all, they smoke marijuana almost every evening to unwind and relieve the tensions of the day. The message from these parents is that it is okay to do drugs.

The Sixtees would be horrified to find out that Sarah and her friends first experimented with marijuana right in their house using their stash. From the time he was ten, Larry helped himself to a few gulps while he was refilling his dad's drink, and Oscar always drank some of his dad's beer when it was left on the table. They all felt a little sneaky and that what they were doing was not quite "right," but it was not all that bad either because their parents were drinking or smoking pot.

Some parents believe that children must be taught to drink responsibly, so they allow them to drink at home. Other parents believe that young people are going to drink, and it is better if they do it at home. Well-meaning parents buy a keg for a son's eighteenth birthday party, never realizing that not all of his friends will be drinking at home, but they will have to get home afterward. Fathers drink beer with their teenage sons while they watch the ballgame on TV. Dad figures it is all right because "He's doing it here with me. I'm teaching him to drink responsibly. Enjoying a beer is part of enjoying the game." Alcohol is so much a part of American life that parents accept its use by young people and signal to them that it is okay to drink.

The attitude that drinking is a phase that all teens go through keeps many parents' eyes closed to the seriousness of a young person's drinking. Many parents minimize alcohol use by saying, "At least she doesn't do drugs." Because alcohol is used by so many parents and other drugs are not, parents put other drugs in a more negative class, apart from alcohol. It eases their minds to think that their son or daughter is *only* drinking.

Today, many parents use marijuana the way they use alcohol; they are simply social users. When they go to a party, they may smoke a joint. That does not make it legal, but it does show the wide acceptance of drug use. For other parents, drug use is so accepted and important that they keep pot or cocaine or whatever chemical they use at home, just as they keep a supply of liquor. Sarah Sixtee is not unusual; lots of young people have gotten high the first time on drugs they have snitched from their parents.

Parents who drink tend to be less concerned when they discover that their sons or daughters drink. If they discover that Son has been using other drugs, they may get excited. If a parent smokes pot or uses other drugs and finds out that Daughter is using, that parent tends to be less upset about it unless Daughter's behavior is interfering with the parent's life in some way. Whatever is familiar tends to be more accepted. Sometimes, even parents who are heavy users of alcohol or drugs get very angry when they discover a son or daughter is drinking or using. They have no idea that they are sending out strong messages that say drinking or using is okay even while they are condemning it in their children.

CONSEQUENCES

Funtime is partytime, and partytime means beer. Hal Hazard started drinking beer early, just like more than half of all seventh graders in the U.S. Although he did not think he had a problem with alcohol, by the time he was in tenth grade Hal was getting drunk at least once a month. He was part of the 30 percent of high school students considered to be abusive drinkers because they get drunk at least six times in one year. Hal and his buddies thought that drinking just made the party fun, unaware that there are more than 3 million teenage alcoholics and problem drinkers in the United States. What was most frightening of all, Hal drove his car after he had been drinking, just as 23 percent of high school students do. He never gave a thought to the fact that the major cause of death in the United States of 15- to 24-year-olds is alcohol. Each year 8,000 teens and young adults,

22 per day, are killed in traffic accidents involving drinking or drugs, and another 40,000 are injured.

Hal had never seen the statistics on alcohol-related problems in our country, but if he had, his reaction would have been, "That won't happen to me. I'm in control." Everyone who is part of the statistics thought the same thing; our prisons, hospitals, cemeteries, and courts are full of them. Even though Hal might ignore the statistics if he saw them, it is hard to overlook the fact that:

- 64% of all homicides are alcohol-related.
- 50% of all traffic fatalities are alcohol-related.
- 50% of deaths by falling are alcohol-related.
- 68% of deaths by drowning are alcohol-related.
- 80% of deaths by fire are alcohol-related.
- 55% of arrests are alcohol-related.
- 60% of child abuse is alcohol-related.
- 60-70% of all violent crime is linked to alcohol and drug abuse.

Society is paying 43 *billion* dollars a year for health care, welfare services, property damage, law enforcement, and absenteeism from work, to say nothing of the high price in lives lost or damaged due to alcoholism or alcohol abuse.

WHO HAS THE PROBLEM?

The problem of chemical or drug abuse belongs to everyone because it affects everyone. Your particular problem may be a parent who abuses drugs (and remember, alcohol is a drug), a brother or sister who gets high all the time, a friend who has begun hanging around the using crowd, a boyfriend who likes to party too much, your desire to be liked but you do not want to do drugs, or your desire to be accepted so you do do drugs. Whatever your problem with drugs, its roots are in our culture, and it is supported by the "do drugs" messages of our pleasure-seeking society that say it is desirable to change the way you feel, that you should never feel uncomfortable.

(Facts presented in this chapter come from the National Institute on Alcohol Abuse and Alcoholism; the National Institute on Drug Abuse; the National Council on Alcoholism; and California State Assembly Bill Number 3016 Fact Sheet on Alcoholism.)

CHAPTER II

Alcoholism and Addiction

A guest speaker from a drug treatment center was coming to Mr. Well's health ed class to talk about drugs and alcohol. No one was particularly excited about it; they expected the usual, "These are the different kinds of drugs and this is what they do to your body; drugs are bad for you; don't do drugs" lecture they had heard since grade school. They were in for a surprise because the speaker, Melanie Mender, believed that studying drugs to learn about addiction was like studying rackets to learn about tennis.

Looking around the room as she started her lecture, Melanie could tell the heavy users by their defiant, hostile looks, and she knew that the students who were trying to look detached and bored might be from families where alcohol and drug abuse were problems. She had seen the same faces many times before and hoped that she could crack their defenses enough to get them to seek help for their own or their families' problems. As she spoke, bored looks began to be replaced with interest.

"It's difficult to talk about substance abuse because abuse has little meaning from a clinical or medical point of view. It's a value judgment. Generally, when the word abuse is used in connection with drugs and alcohol, it means that the person who is using the chemical is behaving in socially unacceptable ways—staggering around, being rowdy in public, fighting with the family. Young people lie and steal to get money for drugs. At work a person may be taking extra long lunch hours or not doing his job as he used to. Mothers sometimes don't take care of their family. When drugs and alcohol are involved, all of these things are considered signs of abuse because the people involved don't seem to value what is considered important to our society.

"We don't like to say the words alcoholism, alcoholic, addiction, or addict. They are not *nice*. Even though it has been thirty years since the American Medical Association recognized alco-

10

holism as a disease, people still behave as though alcoholism or addiction is something to be ashamed of, that only weak, immoral people are alcoholic. Nothing could be further from the truth. People who are alcoholic or addicted to other drugs are very ill. They have a disease that I prefer to call chemical dependency because it has been found that the progression of the disease is the same no matter what chemicals are involved, and many people are polyaddicted—that is, they are dependent on other drugs as well as alcohol. [As she spoke, Melanie looked around the room and saw the usual girl writing the usual note to a friend and the boy whose open folder held a rock magazine.]

"The disease of chemical dependency can be described; it is primary, progressive, chronic, and fatal. Everyone who has chicken pox has a certain set of symptoms that alert the doctor to the disease. Just as the symptoms of chicken pox can be described, so can the symptoms of chemical dependency. Later on I will be describing to you some of the symptoms that show up in the behavior of people who are compulsive users of drugs and alcohol.

"For years drug use was looked on as a symptom of some deep, underlying emotional problem. The overwhelming majority of alcoholics and addicts have no underlying psychological problem, but their lives become unmanageable as a result of their chemical use. Until the chemical use is stopped, it is impossible for them to deal with any of the problems in their lives because the part of the brain needed to deal with those problems is not functioning properly. Some people do have psychiatric problems before they start using, and the chemical is used to self-medicate to escape the pain and discomfort of the mental disease. Their emotional problems become worse as their using progresses, and the drug use must be treated as the primary, or most important, disease until it is stopped; psychiatric problems cannot be effectively treated as long as the person is using. These people are a very small percentage of those considered to be chemically dependent.

"Progressive means that the disease gets worse. It takes a predictable pattern. We see it first in a person's behavior. Later, physical signs become evident. Usually a person uses for quite a while before the body begins to show signs like a bad liver or heart problems. In young people, however, more and more serious physical problems are showing up earlier because their bodies are not growing and developing as they should because of early drug use. Also, when high doses of drugs are mixed together and used, the body can't deal with them. Some young people do permanent damage to their heart with speed, to say nothing of what happens to a brain bathed in alcohol, marijuana, LSD, and whatever. Also, emotional growth is stopped because drug use interferes with a young person's perceptions of the world. A drugged brain can't learn the judgment and decision-making skills necessary for emotional growth. Relationships at home, at school, and in society in general are affected. The behavior of the user becomes more and more unacceptable to others.

"Not only is the disease progressive, but it is also chronic, which means it never goes away. It can be arrested but never cured, and the only means of stopping its progression is by abstinence—not using. Since it can never be cured, if the progression is not stopped, it will be fatal. That doesn't mean that all alcoholics and addicts die as a result of physical complications of their disease, although many do. The third highest killer after cancer and heart disease is alcoholism. However, many addicts and alcoholics don't live long enough for the physical deterioration to happen. They often die violently in car accidents, are shot or knifed during fights, or are killed because they're in the wrong place at the wrong time. Many men are sitting on death row because they killed someone in an alcoholic blackout or when they were loaded on drugs. [As she looked around the class, Melanie noticed that two of the boys she had identified as users looked at each other, and one rolled his eyes, folded his arms across the dripping blood in the picture on his black Iron Maiden T-shirt, and slouched further down in his chair. She smiled grimly to herself as she continued.]

"The disease of chemical dependency has two aspects, and there has been much debate over physical versus psychological dependency. Can a person be an addict if he is only psychologically dependent, or must there be physical dependency for true addiction? Physical addiction has nothing to do with compulsive drug use. The compulsion to use comes about as a result of liking the way you feel when you've used the chemical and being convinced that it can make you feel better. In other words, you use to feel better. It is possible to be psychologically addicted before physical addiction occurs, and that is what usually happens.

"Just as you can be psychologically addicted without being physically addicted, you can be physically addicted without being psychologically addicted. Physical addiction requires that you experience withdrawal symptoms when the drug is stopped. Many people have been on morphine for pain, have gone through physical withdrawal from the drug, and have no desire to use it afterward. When most people think of addiction, they think of physical dependence, and they think of the severe withdrawal symptoms after a long period of use. Psychological dependence is often minimized as being less important in determining addiction. However, Dr. David Knott of the University of Tennessee says that addiction is a behavior disorder that involves getting the drug, using the drug, and trying to remain functional. Psychological dependence comes first and physical dependence later, both working together in chemical dependency.

"Some people don't have problems with either physical or psychological dependence, and that has made researchers ask questions about people's different responses to drugs. Answers are beginning to come in. Research is showing that a large majority of chemically dependent people have alcoholism and drug addiction in their family histories. Sometimes children of alcoholics don't drink, but their children will be alcoholic. In many families there is knowledge of great-grandfathers, grandfathers, grandmothers, fathers, mothers, uncles, aunts, cousins, sisters, and brothers who are all alcoholic or drug-addicted. The genetic factor has definitely been proven. An especially high incidence of alcoholism is found in sons of alcoholic fathers. New research is showing that people with alcoholism in their families, and especially sons of alcoholic fathers, are more likely to become addicted to any chemical, not just alcohol.

"Biologically, chemically dependent people metabolize alcohol and drugs differently from other people. Tests have shown that sons of alcoholic fathers metabolize alcohol differently even if they have never had a drink. Also, electroencephalograph tests measuring electrical activity in the brain show that brain wave patterns of sons of alcoholics are different. As more research goes on with drugs, it is being found that chemically dependent people react biologically to drugs differently because their brain receives the messages from the drugs in a unique way. [Melanie noticed a girl make a comment to her neighbor, and then they both looked at one of the users and giggled silently. She could just imagine what they had to say about his brain.]

"Addiction can't be defined as physical dependence on a chemical or as psychological dependence. Addiction has to do with the impact the drug has on the person's behavior. The relationship between the person and the substance determines how that person functions socially. In chemically dependent people, we see a genetic or biological predisposition to have a different kind of physical relationship with chemicals that encourages the compulsion to use, and usually we find a family pattern of behavior that supports chemical use. Addiction is a bio-psycho-social process.

"All this brings us to the definition of addiction. Addiction is *the compulsive use of a substance with loss of control and continued use of that substance in spite of negative consequences.* In other words, even though the addicts are getting into trouble because of being drunk or high, they continue to use. The negative consequences come in all areas of life—*social*: fights with family, bad grades at school, disruptive classroom behavior, problems at work, arguments with others; *physical*: stomachaches, coughs, runny nose, hangovers, vomiting; *legal*: drunk driving tickets, arrests for assault while drunk or stoned, shoplifting, vandalism, home burglary, runaway; *emotional*: feeling depressed, feeling no good, feeling angry. For addicts, drugs become people substitutes; the addict has a love affair with the chemical rather than with people. So addiction is determined by the impact the chemical has on the person physically and psychologically.

"With so much negative stuff going on, you'd think the addict could see what was happening to him, but the disease of chemical dependency is powerful and is characterized by denial and delusion. The addict does things that are harmful to himself and others and is torn apart inside, but the compulsion to use is so great that he can't stop; he loses control over how much he will use and, finally, whether or not he will use. As more and more goes wrong, he feels worse and worse about himself, and the only way to feel better is to use. He is like a hamster on a wheel, going round and round and not knowing how to stop the wheel and get off.

"Because he believes he is a bad, unworthy person and no one could possibly love him as he is, the chemically dependent person must find a way to make his world bearable. He does that by setting up a defense system whose cornerstone is denial; he simply denies that his using is causing problems. The chemically dependent person or family and friends will say things like: I go to work every day; I can quit anytime I want to; I don't drink any more than anyone else; everybody is getting high these days; the cops had it in for me; with a wife like that I'd drink too; my father drinks more than I do, so why is he getting on my case; he only drinks on weekends; she doesn't use *that* much; I only drink beer; he just likes to party and have a good time. All of those statements are denying the fact that drinking and using are the problem.

"Another brick in the wall of defenses is rationalization. She'll say her son is so hyperactive that she has to have Valium to calm down; he needs a drink to unwind after a hard day; he asserts that it's his body and he's not hurting anyone else; his wife is such a nag that he has to have a few to get through an evening with her; his job is very stressful and he deserves to let down at home; it's her way of relaxing; he wants to be one of the guys; he's too young to be an alcoholic; a little weed just makes you feel mellow. There is always a reason why it's okay to drink or use. [The expressions on several faces in the classroom told Melanie that, as usual, this information had hit home. A dark-haired girl who had been working very hard at being bored and disinterested jerked to attention with a horrified look on her face when she heard the first statements of denial. Melanie made a mental note to keep an eye on her as the lecture went on.]

"Before long the wall grows higher and thicker because the addict sincerely believes his own lies. He can't face his behavior, so he lies about it. He remembers the great time he had at the party but forgets falling down the stairs and causing three other people to fall and spill drinks all over. When someone becomes angry at her outrageous behavior and asks her to leave, she remembers how rude the person was to tell her to leave and sincerely believes she was treated badly. Whenever there is an argument, he tells everyone the other person started it and truly believes that that is what happened. The addict loses touch with what really happened and, in his delusion, thinks that he is okay because he believes what he tells everyone else.

"Because he puts himself in so many negative situations, the chemically dependent person soon begins to feel that the world is against him, and he becomes suspicious of everyone and everything. His growing paranoia causes him to feel alienated from all except his using friends or drinking buddies, but he isn't completely comfortable with them either. The world becomes an unfriendly place full of people who are out to get him. He doesn't realize that he is "getting" himself, but he feels terrible about himself and what is happening in his world. He begins to strike out verbally at others and to accuse them of terrible things; calls them selfish, uncaring; tells them they need to get help because they have problems; tells them they are worthless, no-good, never do anything right; and seems to hate even the people who love him. Family and friends are confused and hurt and don't realize that the alcoholic or addict is projecting all of his horrible feelings toward himself onto other people. He hates himself so much that he accuses others of being the way he sees himself to be but can't admit to himself that he is. It's part of his defense system, and the wall grows higher and thicker. [Melanie glanced at the dark-haired girl, who by now was listening intently.]

"Not being able to see how his behavior is affecting himself and others, the addict blames someone or something else for his problems. If the teachers weren't unreasonable, there would be no problems in class. The principal is a nerd, and that's why he was suspended. His probation officer is to blame for his being in juvenile hall because she turned him in for using. His former friend has problems and got mad over nothing and that's why they don't see each other anymore. Being drunk or stoned never has anything to do with the problem, and the chemical dependent is never to blame for what happened. [Several students turned to look at the boy slouched way down in his seat when the probation officer was mentioned, adding to Melanie's suspicions of his being a user.]

"It is extremely difficult to break through the defense system of denial and delusion, so when someone asks, 'Why don't they see what is happening to them?' the answer is very simple, 'They can't.' They are out of control. It takes intervention from outside to get through the wall. Families and friends can intervene with the help of trained intervention counselors. Alcoholism and drug abuse counselors, staff members of treatment facilities, public health services, and support groups such as the parent support groups who practice the Toughlove philosophy are a few of the people who help families intervene.

"The process of addiction is the same no matter how old you are, but it is speeded up in adolescents because your developing bodies are not capable of handling the harmful effects of the drugs. People who begin to drink regularly in their twenties usually take ten years to get into the chronic stages of alcoholism. Teenagers can become full-blown addicts within a year. Some teens are in trouble with their using from the very beginning. They fail their classes at school, have serious problems with their family and run away from home, get in trouble with the law, give up all their old friends, and become physically messed up all within a single school year. Those whose disease progresses that quickly usually have a family background of alcoholism or addiction. [Melanie noted a few quick glances by students to the back of the room where the users were sitting, looking elaborately unconcerned.]

"Since alcohol is so much a part of our society, let's take a look at some of the misconceptions about alcoholism and explore some of those myths."

At this point, Melanie asked the class to describe an alcoholic. She got the usual answers: someone who drinks all the time; the guys who sleep in the park or in store doorways or alleys; someone who drinks in the morning; someone who can't keep a job; a dirty, scuzzy-looking guy drinking wine out of a bottle in a paper bag.

"All of those things do describe some alcoholics, but they are less than five percent of all the alcoholics in America. Seventy percent of Americans drink, and it is estimated that at least seven percent of all drinkers are alcoholic. Numbers vary, but 11 million is not an overestimation of how many alcoholics are in the United States, with 3.3 million teenage problem drinkers. Who are these 11 million if less than five percent are on skid row? They are your family, friends, neighbors, teachers, doctors, lawyers, plumbers, carpenters, used-car salesmen, grocery store clerks, telephone operators, hairdressers, waitresses, bank presidents, corporation executives, airline pilots, nurses, psychiatrists, drug counselors, students, gardeners, street sweepers, truck drivers, housewives—anyone in any walk of life can be alcoholic. [When Melanie mentioned teachers, there were some quick looks at Mr. Well to see his reaction.]

"Someone said that an alcoholic drinks all the time. Some do, but there are millions who don't. It's not how much you drink or how often you drink, but what happens to you when you drink that is important. People claim that someone can't be an alcoholic because he drinks only on weekends. Does that person get drunk and out of control? When he drinks does he get in fights with his wife, yell and verbally abuse his children, behave in a way that embarrasses people with him? Does he ever feel bad enough to call in sick on Monday morning, or, better yet, have his wife call in sick for him? Does she say that she's going to take it easy and not drink much at the party but end up drunk anyway? Does she forget what she said or did? Do people make comments about his drinking—He was feeling no pain Saturday night. He really tied one on. He likes to have a good time. He can really hold his liquor. All of those things are indicators that, even though he drinks only on weekends, the person is in trouble with his drinking; it's interfering with his life. [At this point, the dark-haired girl was looking very troubled, and a clean-cut boy with glasses was staring fixedly out the window.]

"One of the most vicious forms of alcoholism is found in the binge drinker. These people go for months without drinking, and then go for days or perhaps weeks on a drinking binge that devastates them and their family. When they're drinking you think they must be alcoholic, but they go so long between binges that you are sure they can't be because they don't drink all the time.

"Some people seem to think that someone who drinks only beer can't be an alcoholic. Alcohol is alcohol whether it is beer, wine, or liquor. One beer has the same amount of alcohol as four ounces of wine or one ounce of whiskey. It's not what a person drinks, but what the drinking does to the person that is important. If a man sits in front of the TV drinking a six-pack of beer every night after having had a couple before dinner and falls asleep in the chair night after night, the man is having a relationship with a beer can. If you have any doubt, consider his reaction when he's told there's no more beer in the house. After the smoke of the explosion clears, someone is on the way to the store for beer.

"Another myth about alcoholism is that she can't be an alcoholic because she goes to work every day. The job is nearly always the last thing to go in an alcoholic's life. Her whole world can be crumbling around her, but she will go to work every day. Often co-workers cover and do the work of the alcoholic, trying to be a good friend. It is usually in the final stages of chronic alcoholism that the job goes. Ninety-five percent of all alcoholics are employed or employable, making up five percent of the nation's work force and holding ten percent of the executive positions.

"The alcoholic is not the only one with a strong defense system. Families share the same defense system and can't see what chemical dependency is doing to them. In one survey ninety-eight percent of young people questioned gave parents' fighting as their biggest concern. Only one percent said alcohol was a problem, but how many fights happen when one parent has been drinking? The misconception of who is an alcoholic and the standard reasons given why someone is not are part of a family's and society's denial of the problem.

"Awareness of denial as a defense and knowledge of the disease of chemical dependency can help you look a little more clearly at what is going on in your life. I'm going to tell you a few of the warning signs that dependency might be developing, and, for those of you who are interested, I'll leave some surveys on how to determine if you or someone you care about may have a drug or alcohol problem.

"One of the first signs of a developing problem with chemicals is a desire for a drink or to get high. That becomes, after a while, a need to use at a certain time—need to get high before school; need for a drink after work. The person soon begins to anticipate using as the day goes on. She might say she can hardly wait to get home, put her feet up, and have a glass of wine. He might talk about where he's going after school to get high. You can be aware of how much the person talks about drinking and using and how much he or she looks forward to it.

"Blackouts are a clear warning of problems with alcohol. In one class when I mentioned blackouts and was asked what they were, a student said that blackouts are when your friends tell you what a good time you had last night. [This brought a laugh from the back of the room.] Drinking yourself unconscious is different from having a blackout. During a blackout a person seems to be functioning normally but can't remember what went on. The time is erased from the memory and can't ever be retrieved, not even through hypnosis. Blackouts can be as short as a few minutes and as long as several weeks. An important fact about blackouts is that they are a definite warning sign of alcoholism. Normal drinkers do not have blackouts. [With this, a couple of the back-row laughers looked very serious, and a couple of others shrugged it off with disbelieving looks.]

"Another early warning sign is the development of tolerance. Tolerance is the biological process that demands increased amounts of the drug to get the same effect. You may have heard friends say that once they could get buzzed on one can of beer and now they need at least three to feel anything at all. That's tolerance. The body is adjusting to the increasing use of the drug. Tolerance develops differently with different drugs; it is what tends to get most people into difficulty because they need more and more to feel good. If you could drink two beers or smoke one joint and feel great, you wouldn't have to get loaded and get into all the problems that come from being out of control.

"Often, having a high tolerance is admired. Young people like to brag about how they can *maintain* or how they can *handle it.* Adults at a party comment admiringly how Harvey can drink all night and *never show it.* Those are all clues that someone has a high tolerance, and it is a sign that the person is drinking or using a lot and may be in trouble. [Melanie noticed that several students looked very uncomfortable when they felt someone else's eyes on them.]

"Increasing irritability is often a sign of problem use. The person seems to be in arguments all the time. You can't say anything without its being taken the wrong way. If you say nothing, you're accused of not cooperating or thinking you're too good to take part in the conversation. You do something one day and it's okay, and the next day you get chewed out for the same thing. There seem to be sudden mood changes, and you can't predict what the person's reaction is going to be. You always seem to be wondering what you did wrong. [Now Melanie could see real pain on the face of the dark-haired girl.]

"Those are just a few of the warning signs of problem use. If you have personally experienced them, you may want to look more closely at your own use. If a family member or friend shows any of them, you may want to call the number on the survey forms I'm leaving."

Since it was close to the end of the period, Melanie had time to answer only a few questions before the bell rang. She noticed that over half the students picked up survey forms as they left. Seeing the dark-haired girl pick up a form, Melanie hoped she would call the number at the bottom of the page.

CHAPTER III

Chemical Dependency and the Family

The arguing was louder than usual that night, and as she lay in bed trying to block out the sounds of her parents' angry voices, Joan heard her little brother whimpering as he made his way to her bed. She gave him a hug and whispered that he didn't need to be afraid. Putting him back in his bed, Joan went out to where her parents were arguing. She began to cry loud enough for them to hear before she went into the room, and when they asked what was wrong, Joan told them that she had had a terrible dream and was scared. That would always stop the yelling. [When she got too old to cry over bad dreams, she would just sit by her brother's bed until the yelling stopped or he went to sleep.]

Ever since Joan could remember, her parents had had fights. When she was little, she had asked her mother about the yelling and whether something was wrong. Her mother had told her that everything was fine; there was nothing to worry about. Joan had finally realized that her parents fought when her father had been drinking. As time went on, her father drank every night and often came home drunk. She did not know what to expect. Sometimes her father would be kind and loving, telling her that she was his "little princess," and other times he would tell her she was lazy and never did anything right.

Joan tried very hard to please her father. When she started school, she found that she could do very well. All of her teachers liked her, and she was a hard worker. By the time she was in high school, she was an honor student, she was in the school band, on the track team, editor of the school newspaper, and president of the Spanish Club. When Joan would talk about her activities at school, her mother would say, "That's nice, dear." Her father would ask if she had taken the garbage out. Sometimes her father would look at her report card and make a "humph" sort

22

of noise. Other times he would tell her that she was a chip off the old block, that he used to get straight A's and was an all-city football player.

At home Joan did most of the cooking and cleaning because her mother never seemed to feel well. Joan made sure that the younger kids wore clean clothes when they went to school, that their lunches were made, that they stayed out of her father's way when he was in a bad mood (drunk), but no matter what she did, it was never enough. There was always something else she should have done. No matter how hard she tried, her father would get angry about something. She just could not "get it right."

Teachers thought Joan really "had it together," and she was considered one of the most successful students at school. Other students thought she was smart and talented and confident. She just seemed a little stuck-up, and although she knew most of the other students, she did not have many close friends. There was a group she hung around with, but she never invited anyone to her house and there was no one she confided in. For all of her activity, Joan was really very lonely.

Because of her father's unpredictable behavior when he was drinking, Joan was afraid to invite anyone home. He might do or say something embarrassing, and Joan could not bear the thought of being humiliated in front of a friend. She was afraid that people would not like her if they knew how her father was. She tried so hard to make things better at home, but no matter how hard she tried, things were always a mess. She felt like a total failure, and all of the school activities and academic honors made no difference at all. She was never good enough. She felt lonely and inadequate, guilty about her father's drinking, and angry with her mother for always making excuses for him and then fighting with him all the time. Joan was terribly afraid of her father because he became violent and slapped her mother around sometimes. If the boys were in his way when he was in a rage, her father would push them around too. Joan was afraid that something terrible was going to happen, but she never told anyone how she felt.

Most of the time, Joan covered up her feelings by being involved at school. Never, never did she mention what was happening at home to anyone outside, and never, never did she talk to her brothers about how she felt about her father's drinking. Joan knew that no one outside would understand, and years ago her mother had let her know that her father's behavior was not to be mentioned. Joan was not too sure how she got that message, but she understood it well.

So Joan survived by trying to be perfect so she could please others and gain their approval and feel better about herself, and so her father would not get so angry and drink so much. Funny thing; no matter how much approval she got from outside, Joan still felt bad about herself on the inside, and her father continued to drink more and more. Joan did not know that she was caught in the horrors of the family disease of chemical dependency, and the harder she tried, the more helpless she was to fix her family. Joan was the *family hero.* That was her role in the unfolding drama of alcoholism in her family.

As he walked up to the door, Rick, Joan's brother, knew he was in for it today. He could hear his father in the house, and whenever his father was yelling like that, it meant trouble for him. It seemed to Rick that when he walked in, he became the focus of his father's anger, that anything he had done in the past ten years would be brought up and his father would rant and rave and get himself into a rage. Then the beating would start, and Rick burned with resentment and felt as though he hated his father.

All of his life Rick had been in trouble. He could not remember a time when he did anything right. Before he went to school, he could never seem to do what his parents wanted. Most of the time he was not even sure what he had done to make them angry. One time when he was about four he had been in a big department store and discovered the elevator. He noticed a door slide open and people get off and the door slide closed again. A few seconds later another door slid open and people got off, so Rick ran in before the door closed to see what was going on inside. His mother had not noticed him leave, and when she finally found him an hour later she was so angry that she just jerked him along to the car without saying anything. Plenty was said that night, though, when his father got home, and Rick was very careful where he sat for several days.

Having a perfect sister a year and a half older than he did not make life any easier for Rick. Ever since Rick could remember, Joan had always gotten everything while he got nothing. She was so perfect. His parents were always comparing him to her. "Why can't you sit still the way Joan does?" "Why don't you try hard so you can get good grades the way Joan does?" "Why can't you come in on time the way Joan does?" "Joan never gives us a minute of trouble." His first-grade teacher said, "Oh, you must be Joan's brother. We know you'll do well the way Joan does." In second grade he could tell that his teacher did not expect him to be like Joan because she had already heard about him from his first-grade teacher. By the time he reached his second year of junior high, Rick was getting lectures from his teachers on the first day of school to the effect that any monkey business from him would not be tolerated. Needless to say, his grades were the pits. Why even bother, since he could never do as well as Joan anyway. No matter how hard he tried, he was never as good as Joan in anything, so he stopped trying.

Rick did find that he was good at one thing—getting in trouble. He was always blamed for everything that went wrong. His little brother, Danny, was a real pain, and if Rick so much as looked like he might hit him, Danny would run and tell to get Rick in trouble. Rick could not stand being around the little creep. Whenever Danny did anything wrong, everybody thought it was cute, or they blamed it on Rick and he was punished. He was tired of being hit or grounded or yelled at. Rick felt that no one in the family cared about him and that he was living in a house full of strangers.

His father's drinking bothered Rick a lot. He hated to come home because he never knew whether his father would be drunk. Life at home was never pleasant for Rick, but if his father had been drinking, Rick knew it would be miserable. He would be called punk, stupid, no good, dumb, lazy—and those would be the nice things. Rick had reached the point of saying nothing and looking over his father's right shoulder. That really made the "old man" mad. Rick had learned to keep his mouth shut so as not to get it slapped shut, but he could still put his father into a rage just by looking past him.

Rick's mother was another pain. She was always trying to fix things for his dad, but she never stopped nagging at him. Rick was so tired of her starting in on him as soon as he walked in the door. Lately he just told her where to get off when she made him mad. Almost the only thing she ever did for him was not to tell his father when she was the only one who knew what time he came in. She did not want to "upset Dad," so she would keep her mouth shut about some things. She would sign his deficiency notices and his suspension slips so that his father would not find out. If he wanted a couple of bucks, he could usually talk her out of it. She would try to make him think she was going to tell on him when she wanted him to do something or not do something, and he would tell her to go ahead because she would have to listen to the garbage too. Rick knew she would not tell because she would get her share of trouble for covering for him.

Most of the time Rick stayed out with his friends as much as possible. He was always in trouble for coming home late, but there was no way his parents could control that. Even though they made a big deal out of his being late, he knew they were glad he was not around much. He was not going to stay around and let his father rag on him all the time, especially when the old man was such a miserable drunk. Sometimes Rick thought he hated his father, and his mother made him mad by constantly saying Dad did not really mean it, that he had just had a bad day. Just had a bad day; every day was a bad day for him. Rick's mother was always creeping around trying to "keep the peace" and would never stand up to his father. Rick felt as though he would explode and wanted to strike out at the whole world.

Rick's need to strike out had caused him problems at school, where he had trouble controlling his temper when other students did something to irritate him. He had difficulty with teachers who were always on his back for being late or forgetting his books or not doing his homework. He was not going to put up with their criticism, and he told them what they could do with their books and homework. Consequently, Rick was well known in the school office and had a colorful suspension record.

Lately, Rick had been partying a lot and drinking more and hanging around the drug users at school. They accepted him just as he was and did not expect anything from him. Besides, he was tough and they appreciated that. Nobody was going to push him around, and he would see that nobody bothered them either.

Rick and his buddies would shoplift and trade the stuff they got for drugs. Some of his new friends had done some time in juvenile hall, but they were better at lifting things now, and Rick did not worry about getting caught. He just wanted to get high, because then he felt good and the world looked a lot better. Then he did not have to worry about his drunk and abusive father, his weak and whimpering mother, his pure and perfect sister, or his creepy little brother. He did not have to think about school and teachers on his case or the vice principal who took joy in suspending him. He could just mellow out and enjoy being high and having friends who knew how to be mellow too.

Beneath all of his angry striking out, Rick was very hurt. He did not want to admit it, but he felt lonely and left out, rejected by his family. He felt guilty about the way he treated his mother; he knew that stealing was wrong; he knew he was a mess-up at school. But his anger was so great because he felt his parents did not care about him, because his mother was so easy for his father to manipulate and was always nagging at him, because Joan got everything and he got nothing, because Danny was favored by everyone, because school stank, and because he could never do anything to suit anybody else. He felt like a total mess-up, and he hated himself most of all. So Rick's anger covered up all his feelings of hurt, loneliness, rejection, and guilt.

Rick did not know it, but he was playing out a role in the family disease of chemical dependency. He took the focus away from his father's drinking. Everyone looked at his acting out, and his father's alcoholism took second place. Rick was the *scapegoat*, and his job was to display the pain in his family.

Quietly sandwiched in between Rick and Danny was Robin. She was two years younger than Rick, and she never gave anyone any trouble. Rick just ignored her, and Joan bossed her around if she noticed her at all. If anyone asked Robin's parents about her, their answer was, "Oh, Robin's fine." Actually, they did not know if Robin was fine or not; they never bothered to ask her. She stayed out of the way, did okay in school, and did not get involved in any of the family squabbles. The less people noticed her, the better Robin liked it. That is how it had always been from the time she could remember.

Noisy arguments, angry parents, a resentful brother, a sister who knew everything but shared nothing, confusion and chaos were all that Robin had known. By the time she was born, her father's drinking had become chronic, her mother was busy trying to keep peace in a warring household, Joan was well on her way to making sure that everything was perfect, and Rick was getting lots of attention because he was so "active." No one was particularly interested in Robin. The caring, loving, and nurturing that a new baby needs were not available in her chemically dependent family. Even when she was very tiny, Robin entertained herself and kept herself company. Everyone commented on what a "good" baby she was and then proceeded to ignore her because she was so undemanding.

Stuffed toys and dolls were special friends to Robin. There were even a few imaginary friends who played with her and her animals and dolls. She would sit in a corner of the room for hours playing with her friends because her fantasy world was so much safer than her real world. In her real world, Robin was not important, not worth very much at all. She felt lonely and left out, and what went on in her family was so confusing that it was hard for her to feel a part of things. In her fantasy world she had an important place and a sense of being loved and of belonging.

Because she spent so much time alone, Robin had a hard time making friends when she started school. As she grew up, it was much more satisfying to her to read during recess and lunch than to play games with the other children. She got the feeling of being in a group by singing in the choir, yet she did not draw any attention to herself. Her grades were okay; she never wanted them to be very good and she never let them get very bad because she did not want to be noticed. In elementary school, her teachers did not know much about Robin except that she was very quiet. In junior high, Robin would be in a class for a quarter before the teachers found out her name; if asked about her, they would try to remember the face that went with the name. She seemed to disappear into the woodwork and become invisible, and invisibility suited her just fine.

Wanting invisibility on the one hand to protect herself from the pain in her home, Robin found herself longing to be a part of the world around her on the other; however, she had no idea how to be involved with others. She had no examples of close human relationships at home, had experienced little interaction with adults or other children, and quite simply did not know to become involved with other people. Being alone turned into aching loneliness and feelings of emptiness, confusion, and fear. She was afraid that she would be alone forever and that no one ever could or ever would love her.

Being overweight did not help Robin's feelings of low self-worth, but eating was very comforting. She felt good when she was eating sweet, gooey things like banana splits and toast with gobs of strawberry jam on it.

The only time Robin got any kind of attention from her mother was when she had an asthma attack. Then her mother fussed over her, took her to the doctor, and bought her books or puzzles to make her feel better while she was sick. Robin was the one who fell down and broke her arm when she went roller skating, who fell out of the tree and split open her chin, who tripped on the rug and hit her head on the table and had to have five stitches. Being sick or hurt brought Robin some of the nurturing she needed from her parents, for when she was sick or hurt it seemed that they cared.

Since caring and nurturing came so seldom from others, Robin learned to be very independent at an early age. She could take care of herself and expected little from others; however, she did not see the needs of others and shared little of herself. This made life a lonely place for Robin. She was lost in a confusing world that offered her little understanding or love. Robin was the *lost child* in her chemically dependent family.

Making his appearance three and a half years after Robin was Danny. What a confusing world he came into! Waking to the noisy fights of his parents scared Danny when he was little, and the only one he could turn to was Joan. Although he slept in the same room as Rick, he learned very quickly to leave Rick alone and not cry around him. Rick would tell Danny to shut up and go back to sleep and leave him alone. Danny would creep quietly out of his bed and go into Joan's room. She would always make him feel better, and sometimes she could make their parents stop fighting.

Since he was the youngest, no one ever told Danny what was going on. If he asked questions, they would say that everything was just fine and nothing was wrong. He could feel that things were not right, but he could not figure out what was wrong. Because Danny was so much younger than Joan, she took care of him most of the time when she was not in school. She protected him from Rick's roughness when she could and got on Rick's case when he picked on Danny. Joan also felt that Danny needed protection from the ugliness in the family, so she tried to make things better for him by pretending that fights and arguing did not happen. Joan did not explain things to Danny or tell him about bad things that happened. Joan was not alone in that; their mother would always smile and tell him that he must have had a bad dream or that Daddy was just joking when he raised his voice. It was a very confusing world for Danny, and as he grew older he sometimes wondered if he were going crazy, because what he saw and felt told him one thing while his family told him another. He felt that something must be wrong with him, and that made him feel lonely and inadequate.

Actually what Danny was seeing and feeling was correct, but his family lived by the No-Talk Rule, so no one else would confirm his perceptions. Besides, they all thought he was too little to understand or really notice what was going on. They were too involved in their own survival roles to think about Danny. Being pushed aside and not listened to or taken seriously made Danny feel very unimportant. It also taught him not to trust his feelings and perceptions, and when he got conflicting information from the family, he began not to trust them either. Danny's major feeling most of the time was anxious fear. He was not sure what he was afraid of, but he knew something was very wrong and felt that worse things might happen.

As Danny's anxiety built up, he had to find a way to get relief from the tension in the family. When he was very small, he discovered that if he did something "cute" everyone would laugh. That made Danny feel much better, and it seemed to him that everyone else felt better too. Danny took on the job of making everyone feel good by being funny. He said cute things and did cute things all the time. The only one who seemed to think that Danny was not cute was Rick, and Rick thought he was a real pain. Rick could not stand him because he got so much positive attention, while Rick got the short end of things all the time.

When Danny got into school, teachers did not think he was cute, but the other students thought he was a riot. He was always the class clown. Sometimes his antics interfered with the learning of the other students, and his behavior definitely interfered with his own learning. His attention span was so short that he could not sit still or listen long enough to learn basic skills. In fact, Danny was a typical hyperactive child. With his insides coiled up like a spring ready to bounce, Danny had to release his energy somehow, and he did it by being a human dynamo. He always seemed to be knocking something over, bumping into things, throwing things, running, jumping, talking, humming, buzzing, kicking his feet, waving his arms, bounding, skipping, hopping, splashing, and never still. His bed was a wreck in the morning, so he was not even still in his sleep. Because of his noisy movement, Danny was a constant irritation to some and a comedy to others.

Danny's entertaining was an expression of his nervousness and his efforts to bring his world under control. By keeping people laughing and paying attention to him, he felt much more secure and in control of his confusing world. Actually, Danny did not feel funny at all; he felt afraid. He was afraid that his whole world would fall apart at any moment, that he did not just act crazy, but that he was crazy. He had to keep laughing to keep everyone from knowing how scared he was. Everyone thought that nothing bothered him, while actually everything bothered him. He felt horribly lonely and afraid.

As Danny grew older, he handled everything with a joke or a wisecrack. He never seemed to take anything seriously, including situations that were very serious. Someone's illness was a subject for a joke; an accident meant a joke; getting a poor report card was time to be funny. People may enjoy having clowns around, but they are never taken seriously. Clowns are all right to have around for entertainment, but when peers plan serious activities, clowns are not invited, so Danny was left out. He knew why, and he felt lonely and inadequate; no matter how much attention he got, he still felt unimportant because he knew that no one took him seriously. He often got positive attention, but it was not lasting and did not help him to develop close relationships.

Danny was so busy being a character that he did not have time to develop one. He was not able to attend to the everyday problems of living in a constructive way. If he could not handle a problem by being funny, he did not know what to do. Sometimes his reactions to ordinary situations did not seem to be connected to what was going on at all. He just could not seem to put his mind to solving the simple problems of living. The world was a confusing place to Danny, and low self-esteem along with feelings of fear, loneliness, and inadequacy were the price Danny had to pay for his role as the *mascot* in his chemically dependent family.

ROLES OF CHILDREN IN A CHEMICALLY DEPENDENT FAMILY

Joan, Rick, Robin, and Danny are typical of children who grow up in a family that has an alcoholic or drug-addicted parent. Sharon Wegscheider, in her book *Another Chance*, describes and defines the roles of children in a chemically dependent family, calling them the family *hero*, the *scapegoat*, the *lost child*, and the *mascot*. Not all family heroes are just like Joan, but there are enough similarities to make a hero easy to identify. Some mascots get negative attention rather than positive attention because, unlike Danny, their hyperactivity gets them into trouble. They soon learn that negative attention is better than no attention at all. Since they continually get negative feedback from everyone, they do not feel good about themselves. They really do not want to be bad, but it seems to them that they are, and they suffer from low self-esteem along with feelings of fear, loneliness, and inadequacy just as the happy-go-lucky clowning family mascot does.

The scapegoat of the family usually gets his role because the hero position is already taken; knowing he can never be as good as the hero in anything, he decides to be the best at being bad. Sometimes the eldest child becomes the scapegoat when the second child, who becomes regarded as perfect, is born. Whichever way the hero and scapegoat fall, there is always one who gets the focus of the negative attention, who seems to make everyone angry, and who seems to be able to do nothing right.

Somewhere in the middle of the family comes the quiet one like Robin who seems to get lost in the bustle and the turmoil. If Mother talks about her children, she will brag about the hero, complain about the scapegoat, and say that the mascot is a handful but never mention the lost child. If someone should ask about the lost child, the answer is always, "Oh, she's just fine; never gives us any trouble at all."

Children in chemically dependent homes are trapped in their roles as the only means of survival in that family system. If things were to be different, the family members would have to be open and discuss honestly what is happening in the family. The most powerful unspoken rule in a chemically dependent family is the No-Talk Rule, and the lack of talk creates the necessity for having a role in order to survive. No one dares to show the real person behind the mask, because the real person would feel the pain if the mask were gone. Besides not talking about what is happening in the family, it is extremely important not to feel the pain and frustration that come from living with the dishonesty, uncertainty, anger, guilt, loneliness, and horrible tension that are created in a chemically dependent home. Not talking and not feeling create the delusion that things are okay, and having a role to play and hide in makes it possible to survive.

PARENTS IN A CHEMICALLY DEPENDENT FAMILY

Jim and Carol Swig, married when they were twenty-four and twenty, enjoyed socializing with their friends. Jim had always been able to "hold his liquor," so socializing meant drinking. Every once in a while Jim would lose control and do something that was embarrassing to Carol, or they would have an argument when he had had too much to drink. As time went on, the arguments became more frequent because Carol would complain about Jim's embarrassing behavior or his being late for dinner because he had stopped to "have a few" with the guys.

When Joan was born, it became more difficult for Carol to

party with Jim, so he began going out by himself. He would come home drunk, and Carol would be angry because she had stayed up worrying about him, afraid he had been in an accident because he was so late. There would be a terrible fight, but the next morning Jim would act as if nothing had happened. Sometimes he would have such a hangover that he would tell Carol to call his boss and say he had a little touch of the flu.

By the time Robin came on the scene, Jim was doing very little with his family. He complained that Rick was so noisy and such a nuisance that watching TV or reading the paper was impossible. Besides, Carol had become such a nag that she was no fun to be around. All she thought of was the kids, as far as Jim could see. All he heard was complaining that there was never enough money, and if he bought a case of beer on the weekend for when he watched the ball game and worked around the house, she had a fit about it. No wonder he spent more and more time away from home, and she complained about that too.

As time went on, Jim became more and more distant. His behavior at home became unpredictable; one minute he was in a good mood and everything was fine, and then someone would say or do something to set him off and he would be in a rage. Sometimes he would promise to take Rick fishing on the weekend, then completely forget about it and do something with his own friends instead. Instead of mowing the lawn, Jim would sit and drink with the next-door neighbor and then yell at Rick for not doing the yard work. Carol would defend Rick, and that would be an excuse for Jim to fight with her or to stomp out and come home drunk.

The broken promises, sudden unprovoked rage, and other unpredictable behavior were confusing and painful for the family. They were sure that Jim did not care about them. How could he forget that he had said he would take Rick fishing, that he would go to Joan's band concert, that he would attend Robin's school open house, that he would take Danny to the circus? How could he possibly forget that he had slapped Carol during a fight the night before? How could he say that it was too bad the neighbor's prize rose bush was crushed and ask how it happened when the whole neighborhood had heard him yelling last night that it was in his driveway and deserved to be run over if they were going to plant it in his way? He just did not care about anything or anybody. What other possible explanation could there be?

When people told Jim that he had said and done things he did not remember, he tried not to believe them, to think that they were making it up to make him feel bad. After a while, Jim realized that he actually was saying and doing things that he did not remember. Jim was experiencing alcoholic blackouts. Some mornings when he read a report in the paper about a hit-and-run accident, he would go to the garage and check his car to see if he might have been the driver. Blackouts were becoming a nightmare for Jim, but he could not tell anyone about them because they might think he was crazy or that his drinking was becoming a problem. So Jim's defense was to get angry and blame everything on others; to give excuses and make up lies until he believed the lies and distrusted those he blamed.

While the family felt afraid of Jim's anger, guilty from his blaming, and distrustful from his lies, Jim felt worthless, guilty, shameful, and unlovable. There was so much pain that Jim drank to cover his feelings and lied to himself by blaming others and never taking responsibility for his behavior. When something particularly serious happened as a result of Jim's drinking, he would "go on the wagon" and stop drinking for a time. Sooner or later, however, a problem would come up at home or at work that Jim would use as an excuse to drink again, and once he started drinking, he lost control. Jim hated himself and felt so lonely and worthless that he had to work harder at covering up those feelings, becoming more and more angry and blaming, and making rigid rules for others to protect himself from feeling.

The Nondrinking Parent

At the time of her marriage, Carol was a legal secretary for two attorneys and enjoyed the independence that her salary and her own self-confidence gave her. She decided to continue working until they had a family so she and Jim could buy a house and furniture and have a few years of enjoying each other before they settled down to the more serious business of raising a family.

Carol wanted everything to be perfect for her family, since her own young years had been awful because her father drank too much and her mother had to support the family of five children. They never had enough money for fun things, and Carol had begun helping her mother support the family by baby-sitting as soon as she was old enough for neighbors to trust her.

Because she was so reliable and dependable, Carol had no difficulty getting a real job as soon as she was sixteen. She took business classes in school, and her office skills were so good that, shortly after graduation, she was recommended to a friend of her teacher who was just beginning his law practice in a nearby town. Hating to leave her mother but needing to get out of the miserable situation at home, Carol took the job with a sigh of relief.

When Jim Swig came into her life, he was so fun-loving and full of life that she did not notice that most of his social life was partying. He had so many friends and did so many fun things that Carol got caught up in the gaiety and exuberance of people such as she had never known before. They were all just a little older than she and so much more sophisticated that she felt honored to be accepted by them. She had no experience with drinking other than her father's overindulgence. Carol had stayed away from booze and the "drinking crowd" in school. She had no desire to become like her father, or like her mother for that matter. Since Jim did not get drunk and ugly like her father, Carol knew he did not have a drinking problem, so she decided to enjoy the social drinking and would occasionally wake up with a headache herself.

The first time Jim embarrassed Carol when he had had too much to drink, she decided that no one else seemed to be upset so she would just forget it. After they had been married a few years, it seemed that Jim was doing and saying embarrassing things at every party, and she always seemed to be apologizing or making excuses for him. When he was hung over, she called his boss to say he was not feeling well.

Shortly before Joan was born, Carol quit her job to be a full-time mother. By this time, she and Jim were quarreling regularly because of his behavior when he had been drinking. After Joan was born, the quarreling increased because Carol was so busy with her baby that Jim felt she was neglecting him. Carol did her best to satisfy Jim in every way, but she always seemed to fall short. Jim would get angry, tell her she was a nag and never did anything right, and stomp out and spend the evening in a bar. Sometimes when he got home he would apologize and be very loving toward Carol, and sometimes he would be more belligerent than when he had left. Carol was sure she was not doing the right things to keep Jim happy and that that was why he was drinking so much.

As time went on and babies were born, Carol felt as though more and more responsibilities were being piled on her. Jim was spending too much money on liquor and nights out, and she was having to make excuses for late bills. Finally, Carol decided to go back to work. She was tired of arguing over money and trying to cover up Jim's extravagances. she was tired of bearing the brunt of his bad temper and being blamed for every little thing that went wrong, and she had begun to be afraid of him because he had begun pushing her around and even slapping her.

Carol tried her best to keep the fights and ugliness away from the children, especially Danny because he was so little. Joan was so wonderful about helping around the house that Carol did not know what she would do without her. Working so hard at the office and coming home to the unpredictability of Jim's moods and behavior were taking their toll on Carol. She began to have headaches, and her stomach bothered her. She was constantly tired. She could never get a good night's sleep because of her worry when Jim was out or the fighting when he was home. He used to have periods when things seemed to be better and he treated her better, but lately it was just one long battle royal.

Carol was totally worn out and just did not have any patience for anyone. Rick accused her of nagging and complaining all the time. He really was getting to be more than she could handle, but she would not say anything to Jim because he would use it as an excuse to berate and hit Rick. Carol would do anything she could to keep peace in the family.

In spite of everything she did, Carol felt helpless and inadequate. She felt guilty because Jim blamed her for his drinking, and nothing seemed to help no matter how hard she tried. She was angry because she was not appreciated, but she kept her angry feelings bottled up inside because she knew it would do no good to say anything to Jim; it would only make matters worse. Sometimes, though, Carol was so full of resentment that she could not hold it in, and there would be an outburst of anger.

Carol was afraid that she might not be able to hold things together, afraid that Jim would get worse and lose his job, afraid that the children were being hurt by the fights and Jim's attitude toward them, afraid of being afraid. Sometimes the situation seemed hopeless. She tried so hard to make everything work out, but Jim only got worse.

Carol was caught in the trap of chief enabler. Everything she did only made it easier for Jim to continue drinking. He did not have to face the consequences of his drinking because Carol fixed everything. She apologized for him; she made sure the bills were paid; she put the car in the driveway when he parked it in the middle of the lawn; she put him to bed when he passed out in the living room; she made excuses and refused invitations so others would not find out how obnoxious Jim had become when he got drunk; she went to all the school concerts and teacher conferences; she took the car in for repairs; she bought a "how to" book and fixed the leaking faucets. Carol became mother and father to the children and took over all the responsibilities of the home. Jim did not have to do a thing because Carol cleaned up his messes and made up for most of his neglect. She enabled him to continue drinking, all the while thinking she was doing her best to make him stop because she pleaded with him to stop, refused to give him any money, emptied his bottles when she found them, and did her best to make him understand what he was doing to himself and the family.

All Carol got for her efforts was anger and fear and feelings of self-hatred and guilt because she was incapable of controlling the drinking. Her feelings of low self-worth were so overwhelming that she, too, shut off her painful feelings, and with them all of her loving feelings as well. She blamed Jim for all her troubles and began berating him for mistreating her and the children. Her anger, held in for so long, could no longer be contained, and Carol became a persecutor of the man she felt was causing her unhappiness.

THE FAMILY DISEASE OF
CHEMICAL DEPENDENCY

Everyone in the Swig family was reacting to Jim's behavior. Their whole world revolved around his moods, rages, and unpredictable behavior; they adjusted to survive in that family system. They could not express their true feelings, so they played out their roles, hoping that others would not know how desperate they felt and hoping they could forget the pain that drove them into the roles.

Because the family must adjust to the behavior of the chemically dependent person to survive, that adjustment requires the family to react and adjust to one another as well. The more trouble Rick got into, the more perfect Joan felt she had to be and the more Robin wanted to disappear. The more perfect Joan became, the angrier Rick got and the meaner he became toward Danny. The meaner Rick became, the more Danny wanted to get even, so he would tell on Rick. The more confusion that went on in the house, the more Robin retreated to her fantasy world.

The angrier Carol got, the more she took it out on Rick and Danny as well as Jim. Rick saw her as the persecutor and did not blame his dad for drinking when his mother was like that. Joan saw her father as the persecutor and hated the way he treated her mother, who was working so hard to keep things together. Joan also saw Rick as persecuting her mother. Danny just saw things as totally confusing, and the more jokes he could make to relieve the tension, the better. Robin took care of herself and ate. And Jim saw everyone against him and no one giving him any support at all; no wonder he had to drink.

Everyone in the family suffered from Jim's alcoholism. They all had the disease too, even though they were not drinking. They were so consumed by him and his behavior that their lives revolved around him. They were what is known as *codependent*. Jim was the dependent; he was dependent upon alcohol. The family became so focused on him that they were, in a real sense, addicted to or dependent upon him for their identities. His alcoholism ruled their lives. How everyone felt depended on how Jim felt. Everyone worried about how he would react to any situation. They all felt like failures because they could not meet Jim's or their own expectations. They felt guilty because of his behavior and did not want anyone to know how horrible things were in their family. For them, co-dependency had become a life-style, a pattern of living.

Not all chemically dependent families are exactly like the Swigs; however, the behavior patterns can be found. Women are frequently alcoholic or dependent on other drugs. Women particularly may be addicted to prescription drugs such as tranquilizers, sleeping pills, or painkillers. When the mother is the dependent, the father takes over many of her duties and does the covering up so "people won't know," but he has the same feelings as Carol. Usually, husbands do not stay with wives who are chemically dependent; they leave or get a divorce. Women are far more likely to "stick it out" than men.

If there are only two children in the family, the roles may look a little different, and one child may take on two roles. The hero may also feel responsible for keeping the tension down and be a mascot at times. The scapegoat may retreat into the lost child, or he may be pretty funny some of the time. Usually, a child is mainly in one role, with another as a "sideline." An only child may be forced to take on all of the roles. What a confusing life that can be! In large families, two children may assume one role, because when all roles are taken, duplication becomes necessary. After a period of time in any role, the person gets caught in it, and the rigidity of the chemically dependent family makes it impossible to get out. The No-Talk and Don't-Feel Rules keep the person in the role, and the inability to trust self and others may keep him or her in the role even as an adult. Millions of people who are adult children of alcoholics are still suffering the pain of growing up in a chemically dependent home. The National Association of Children of Alcoholics, 31706 Coast Highway, Suite 201, South Laguna, California 92677, is an organization that recognizes and understands the needs of children of alcoholics of all ages.

CHAPTER IV

Coping with a Parent Who Drinks

Her hand was trembling so that Joan Swig could hardly
dial the telephone. She knew she had to do it because she was so
confused and so scared that she thought she was going crazy,
and she had to have answers to some of her questions or she
would go crazy. Ever since Melanie Mender, the woman from
the treatment center, had talked about alcoholism last week in
her health ed class, Joan had been fighting what she now knew
to be true. As she held the survey "Is There a Drinking Problem
in Your Family?" to get the phone number, she looked at it once
more.

IS THERE A DRINKING PROBLEM
IN YOUR FAMILY?

yes	no	1.	Do you worry about your parent's drinking?
yes	no	2.	Have you ever been embarrassed by it?
yes	no	3.	Are holidays more of a nightmare than a celebration because of your parent's drinking?
yes	no	4.	Are most of your parent's friends heavy drinkers?
yes	no	5.	Does your parent often promise to quit drinking without success?
yes	no	6.	Does your parent's drinking make the atmosphere in the home tense and anxious?
yes	no	7.	Does your parent deny having a drinking problem because he or she drinks only beer?
yes	no	8.	Do you find it necessary to lie to employers, relatives, or friends to hide your parent's drinking?
yes	no	9.	Has your parent ever failed to remember what happened during a drinking period?
yes	no	10.	Does your parent avoid conversation pertaining to alcohol or problem-drinking?

41

yes   no   11. Does your parent justify his or her drinking problem?

yes   no   12. Does your parent avoid social situations where alcoholic beverages will not be served?

yes   no   13. Do you ever feel guilty about your parent's drinking?

yes   no   14. Has your parent driven a vehicle while under the influence of alcohol?

yes   no   15. Are you and your brothers or sisters afraid of your parent while s/he is drinking?

yes   no   16. Is your other parent afraid of physical or verbal abuse when your parent has been drinking?

yes   no   17. Has another person mentioned your parent's unusual drinking behavior?

yes   no   18. Do you fear riding with your parent when s/he has been drinking?

yes   no   19. Does your parent have periods of regret after a drinking occasion and apologize for unacceptable behavior?

yes   no   20. Is less alcohol required now for your parent to bring about the same effects that more alcohol did in the past?

If you have answered yes to any two questions, it is a definite warning that a drinking problem may exist in your family. If you answered yes to any four questions, the chances are that a drinking problem exists in your family. If you answered yes to five or more questions, there is definitely a serious drinking problem in your family.

Joan stared at the survey and the sixteen yeses on it. If five mean a serious drinking problem, what must sixteen mean? She had gone over and over the survey to see if she could talk herself out of some of the yeses.

1. Did she worry?—Oh, boy! Did she worry! What would it be like not to worry about Dad killing himself and someone else driving home drunk? (That's 14 that gets a yes too, and of course 18 because of being afraid to ride with him herself.) What would it be like not to have to worry that he would hurt someone in the

family when he comes home roaring drunk and in a rage? (That's 15 and 16.) What would it be like not to have to worry that her friends might find out how awful he acted? She felt so guilty about his behavior that she was afraid no one would like her if they knew how he was, so she lied about him all the time. (Let's see, that takes care of questions 8 and 13.)

2. Have I ever been embarrassed by Dad's behavior?—Just thinking about the time he came to the track meet drunk made her turn red and uncomfortable, and there was the time he tried to put his arm around her friend Kellie while he was saying what a "cutie" she was. Talk about embarrassed!

3. Are holidays a nightmare?—You bet! All of Dad's drinking buddies drop by for a little "holiday cheer"—lots of cheer there. Dad gets obnoxious and never remembers what he says or does (That's numbers 4 and 9 too), and if we go to visit family or friends who don't have lots of booze around, he grumbles for days afterward and swears he'll never go there again because they're too cheap to serve more than two drinks. (Oh, boy, that's number 12.)

5. Does he promise to quit drinking?—Well, he promises to cut down all the time and never does. She decided not to check this one because she was not sure.

6. Does his drinking make the atmosphere tense and anxious?—Well, she had not thought before that it was his drinking particularly, because it was tense and anxious when he was around whether he'd been drinking or not, but it was worse when he had been drinking, so she had to check yes on this one.

7. Her father drank liquor, so she could skip the one about only drinking beer.

10. Does he avoid conversation about alcohol or problem-drinking?—The family never talked about alcohol or drinking to him or to each other, so she decided to skip this one too.

11. Does he justify his drinking?—Her mother made excuses for him: How hard he works for us; he has so many worries; he didn't mean to hurt Rick; he didn't really mean what he said—Joan wanted to scream just thinking about it!

12 to 16 are checked off already.

17. Has another person mentioned his drinking?—How about, "Your Dad's really different when he's drinking," or,

"Gee, your Dad can really hold his liquor. Everybody I know would pass out if they drank that much." It was embarrassing even to think about it.

19. Does he have periods of regret and apologize?—That was another one to add to embarrassment. It would be better just to forget about it sometimes than to listen to his apologies. Besides, what good are the apologies when he does the same things over and over?

20. Does it take less alcohol for him to get drunk?—Who knows how much he drinks before he gets home? She really did not know the answer to that one.

Any way Joan looked at the survey, it added up to sixteen yeses. She listened to the ring at the other end and almost put the phone down, but her need for help was stronger than her fear. Even so, she had to clear her throat and start over when she asked for Melanie Mender. Joan knew that her voice was trembling when she told Melanie she was a student in Mr. Well's health ed class, and she was surprised when Melanie asked if she were the dark-haired girl sitting in the middle of the room across from the tall blond boy. In one sense Joan liked the idea that Melanie had noticed her, but in another she had hoped to ask her questions and not be known. Joan got another surprise when she heard herself agreeing with Melanie's invitation to come to her office so they could spend some time talking about whatever Joan wanted to discuss.

Three days later, sitting in a rocking chair in Melanie's office, Joan told her about the survey. With the understanding she could see in Melanie's expression, it was as though a dam burst, and Joan could not stop talking once she started. She told about her parents' fighting and how scared she was that her father would hurt her mother because he had begun to shove her around the way he did her brother Rick. She told how her father made promises that he never kept; how he told people things she knew were not true; how things would be all right one minute and he would be in a rage the next; how hard she tried to do everything he wanted and expected so that he would not be angry, and how he would always find something to get mad about anyway. Joan told how hurt she was when she had won a second-place trophy at the state track meet, and her father only wanted to know why she had not come in first. She had ended up feeling guilty and ashamed for not doing as well as her father expected.

After almost a half hour of talking nonstop and rocking in the rocking chair, Joan finally said that she had been afraid for a long time that her father might be an alcoholic, but it was not until Melanie had talked about denial and rationalization that she saw that the excuses she made for her father were just covering up what she knew to be true. With that, Joan burst into tears and cried and rocked and cried and rocked. Melanie handed her a box of tissues and gently told her that it was okay to cry.

Even though Joan's story was an old one to Melanie, the fear, hurt, guilt, shame, and disappointment were as painful for Melanie to hear about as the first time she had heard the story of a child of an alcoholic. She knew the destruction and devastation that alcoholism cause in a family, and she knew how difficult it was for Joan to break the No-Talk Rule and tell the family secrets.

As Joan quieted down, Melanie began to talk about some of the matters that she knew Joan needed answered. She told Joan that her father did not want to hurt his family, did not want to embarrass them by his behavior, did not want to drink the way he did. The compulsion to drink was so great that it was the most important thing in his life; he could not admit that he drank too much and that his drinking was out of control. He felt so guilty and worthless as a result that he drank more to cover up his bad feelings.

When Joan wanted to know why her father could not see what was happening, Melanie reminded her about denial—that not seeing is how people protect themselves. Joan was just beginning to recognize her own denial of her father's drinking problem and how it affected her life, so she could understand how very strong her father's denial must be.

Not wanting to admit that his drinking was causing problems in his life was one thing, but Joan could not understand how he could treat the family the way he did. He said such terrible things about everyone. He called her mother and brother horrible names, told them they were no good. He accused her mother of awful things that Joan knew could not possibly be true. Melanie explained that her father was "projecting" all of his bad feelings about himself onto other people. He felt so miserable inside that he called other people all the names he wanted to call himself and accused them of things that, perhaps, he had done. Instead of thinking, "How could he say that to *me*?" Joan needed to realize that he was not saying it to hurt her, personally. His striking out was a part of his disease, and whoever happened to be there would be on the receiving end. Families get the most abuse because employers and friends do not have to put up with that kind of behavior, so the alcoholic takes out his frustrations and self-hate on his family.

Something that particularly bothered Joan was her feelings toward her father. At times she hated him, and she felt guilty because you are not supposed to hate your parents. On the other hand, she really loved her father; he was very important to her. She felt torn apart by her feelings. Melanie understood what Joan was talking about; she suggested that it was her father's behavior that Joan hated, that certainly no one could be expected to like someone who ranted and raved, called people names, and was generally disagreeable. Melanie pointed out that if anyone else treated her and her family the way her father did, she would not like that person either. Joan agreed with that and felt better when she realized that it was okay to have those feelings and that she could still love her father at the same time.

Just saying things out loud to Melanie seemed to help Joan. They did not seem so scary once they were in the open. Once she found out that it was not unusual to have conflicting feelings about a parent, she realized that sometimes she did not like the way her mother acted either. She wanted to know why her mother was so short-tempered and grouchy and mean. It seemed that she was yelling at someone or about something all the time. Melanie explained that her mother was taking out her anger at her husband on the rest of the family, and that she was dealing with her extreme stress in the only way she knew how. When Joan thought about it, it made sense; she did not like it, but it made sense. Maybe her own irritability with her mother was a result of the tension in the house. She decided that maybe if she were a little less "snappy" toward her mother it might help things a bit.

Another thing that bothered Joan was her mother's lack of attention to her and her sister and brothers aside from arguing with them. It seemed that her mother just wanted them to stay out of the way, that she focused all her attention on trying to please their father. Her mother was always making excuses for her father; she was constantly worried about him when he was late and sometimes went out looking for him. Joan felt that her mother never paid attention to what was going on with the rest of the family. Melanie explained to Joan that her mother was as obsessed with her father as he was with drinking. In fact, Joan realized when it was pointed out, the entire family revolved around the moods and whims of her father.

Sensing that Joan had not told her everything that was going on, Melanie mentioned that if any physical violence was going on in the family it was very important that she get to a safe place. Joan wondered how Melanie knew so much about her family, not realizing that violence is part of the pattern in an alcoholic home. Even though it seemed extreme, Joan paid attention when Melanie told her to call the police if she were afraid for the safety of anyone in the house. The fact that Joan had to do such a thing might be what her father needed to make him realize that his drinking was out of control.

Even though Joan had not mentioned it, Melanie knew that Joan felt somehow to blame for her father's drinking. Because the alcoholic parent says things like, "Nobody around here cares what I think anyway," or "Why is it I have to get mad before anybody does anything around here?" children think that they are causing their parent so much distress that it causes the drinking. Chores not done around the hourse, one B with four As, a fight with a brother do not cause a disease, Melanie reminded Joan. One of the alcoholic's symptoms is finding someone to blame for his troubles, and family members are the handiest people to blame. Joan had been trying for a long time to be as perfect as possible for her father, and she was relieved to find out that she was not the cause of his anger and drinking. She knew it would help to remember that she could not cause a disease.

Melanie said that there were three Cs for Joan to remember. She did not *cause* the disease, she could not *control* it, and she could not *cure* it. Even though Joan had not realized what she was doing, she had tried to control her father's drinking. When he told her to fix him a drink, she always went very light on the liquor. When he was not paying attention she would take his glass into the kitchen and empty it. She had even emptied bottles when she did not want him to drink anymore that night. None of those things worked; he would always find a bottle he had stashed somewhere, would refill the emptied glass, or complain about the weak drink and pour more liquor into it. Joan had read articles about how futile it was to empty liquor out of bottles, but she thought that since she was not looking for hidden bottles and emptying them, she was okay. She felt a little silly about it until Melanie reminded her that it was part of her denial to think that the bottles she emptied were different.

Joan was willing to admit that she could not cure her father, but she did not want to give up on him either. She felt that if she tried harder, perhaps she could keep from making him so angry; and maybe since she had never asked him to stop drinking, he might think about it if she did ask. Maybe if she told him how terrible things were with the family he would stop. Very gently Melanie explained that there was no way to force someone to see that his drinking was getting him into more and more trouble. An alcoholic cannot stop drinking until he wants to, until the pain caused by the drinking is worse than the pain he is trying to cover up. However, Melanie told Joan that there were some things she could do for herself that would make it less difficult for her.

When her father had been drinking, Joan learned, it was best not to try to reason with him. When he accused or blamed or demanded, it was best to say nothing or as little as possible. When her father was very belligerent and wanted a fight, it would be difficult to keep from getting caught up in it; however, if Joan had to say something, a simple remark like, "I'm sorry you feel that way," might avoid the fight. Once the alcoholic gets started, the fights last for a long time.

If Joan had an issue to discuss with her father, she was advised to wait until morning or a time when she knew he had not been drinking before bringing it up. Talking to her father when he had been drinking did as much good as talking to the bottle he had been drinking out of. When she did get caught up in something with him when he was drinking, she had to keep reminding herself that her father had a disease and that what he was saying was not really true; it was the alcohol talking.

The embarrassing incident when her father put his arm around her friend had caused Joan to stop inviting friends to her house. Understanding how humiliating that could be, Melanie told Joan that she was not responsible for her father's behavior and need not be ashamed. His disease caused the behavior. Melanie knew that Joan wanted to be proud of her father, and that his behavior hurt her very much. However, it was important to remember that he did not mean things personally and that he was not trying to hurt her. Her father's compulsion to use alcohol in spite of negative consequences was caused by his disease of alcoholism. It did not make him a bad person. She did not have to feel embarrassed by his behavior or guilty or ashamed. When those feelings came up, Joan could tell herself that her father had a disease.

Breaking the No-Talk Rule would be the most freeing thing that Joan could do, Melanie said. If Joan could explain to her friends about alcoholism, about how unpredictable her father's behavior was and how he sometimes did embarrassing things, her friends would be understanding. In fact, Melanie assured Joan, her friends already knew about her father. They felt uncomfortable because Joan had not talked about it, and they did not want her to feel worse than she already did. They knew that she had no control over her father's drinking, and it was unlikely that they blamed her for his behavior. Talking about her father's drinking would make it easier for everyone.

Breaking the No-Talk Rule in the family was important, too. Everyone knew that the fights between her parents were much worse when her father had been drinking. Everyone knew that he was drunk when he parked the car in the middle of the lawn. The whole family knew when he fell on the living room floor that her father had passed out because he was drunk, and everyone pretended not to notice. Joan was afraid that her father would have an accident and kill himself or someone else driving home some night. She needed to share her concern with her mother. When her mother made excuses for her father's behavior, Joan could say, "Dad left the car on the lawn because he was drunk. I'm not being mean, Mom, I'm trying to be honest." Melanie suggested that when Joan and her mother were alone and calm, Joan could say, "Mom, I'm really worried about Dad's drinking."

Knowing it would be very difficult for Joan to break the No-Talk Rule, Melanie gave her an idea for something a little less difficult. Telling Joan that her father needed to know that he was loved, she suggested that Joan go to him at a time when he had not been drinking and say, "Dad, I just want you to know I love you." Because alcoholics' self-esteem is so low and they truly believe that no one could love them, they desperately need to hear that they are loved. Joan tried to think of the last time she had told her father that she loved him, and she could not remember for sure when it was. He had not told her he loved her either, but Melanie urged her not to let that stand in her way.

Joan's look of being weighed down with doom and gloom had lightened a little, and Melanie suggested that she come back another time and talk some more after she had had an opportunity to think about the things they had talked about. In the meantime, Melanie recommended that Joan attend a meeting of Alateen, the support group for teenagers who had lived or were living with an alcoholic. She gave Joan a list of the meeting times and places and a phone number to call if she wanted a ride.

When they met a week later, Joan told Melanie that she had tried to work on not blaming her father for his drinking and telling herself that his disease was doing the talking when he said awful things. It had helped a little, and she was trying hard not to take things personally. She had thought a lot about the three Cs, and even though she knew she could not cure his disease, Joan wanted to do something to help her father stop drinking.

When Melanie asked if she had talked to her mother, Joan admitted that she had not been able to mention her father's drinking to anyone. She had not gone to an Alateen meeting either, and Melanie told her that the most helpful things she could do were to break the No-Talk Rule and to go to Alateen. They practiced what Joan might say to her mother, and Joan decided she could start by simply saying, "Mom, I'm worried about Dad's drinking." For the time being, she would leave it at that and see what her mother said. She also made a commitment to go to an Alateen meeting.

Since there had been violence in the family, Melanie worked out a safety plan with Joan. Knowing how difficult it would be to call the police, Melanie asked if there were any relatives in town she could call if she were afraid. Joan said she could call her Uncle Jay, her father's brother, because she knew that he did not like the way her father acted when he had been drinking. Joan also agreed to call the police if she could not get in touch with her uncle. She made a list of numbers that she would keep handy in case of emergency. Joan suddenly started to cry, and when Melanie asked her what she was feeling, Joan said that on Saturday night she had been so scared that she almost called the police. She wished she had thought about calling her Uncle Jay then.

When Joan asked if there were not something more that could be done to make her father stop drinking, Melanie told her about a process called intervention in which a family can take part to make the alcoholic aware of how bad things are getting. It has to be done very carefully with a trained counselor. The purpose of the intervention is to get the alcoholic to seek help; it could be getting him to agree to go into a treatment facility or to see an alcoholism counselor. The family must be very thoroughly prepared by the intervention counselor or else the alcoholic's denial can be reinforced by an unhelpful confrontation.

After talking more about intervention, Joan decided that she would work toward getting her mother to meet with Melanie. She was determined to break the No-Talk Rule. That had to be done before anything else could happen with her family. Knowing that she would need all the support she could get, Joan decided to go to Alateen as soon as possible. Talking to other teens who were struggling with the same problems would help her. She had not wanted to go before because she thought that anyone who went there must be a loser. From listening to Melanie, however, Joan realized that if she were to find winners in the war against alcoholism, Alateen was the place to look. She left the center that day with more hope than she had felt in a long time.

COPING WITH A PARENT WHO DRINKS

Living in the unpredictability of an alcoholic home is a nightmare for children. They become so weighed down with secrets that it is hard to think of anything else. They may have difficulty in school because they cannot concentrate—paying attention in class may be a real problem; forgetting things will upset adults; teachers may get very frustrated and complain. It is hard to put the cares of home aside while at school.

For other children, school becomes a haven. It is the place where they can do well, can "get it right," can be successful. They may choose academic excellence, or they may get involved in other activities. Some children of alcoholics do everything—academics, sports, music, student government. They may be cooking, cleaning, washing clothes, and taking care of the younger children as well. Some get jobs early on. They become overachievers to keep their minds off of how they feel about what is going on at home and to make up for their feelings of inadequacy about not making things better.

Having a mother who drinks too much can produce some special problems, because as a rule men leave alcoholic wives. Often children are left to deal with the drinking parent without their father's support. If your mother drinks too much, you may feel obligated to take care of her. You do the cleaning and the cooking if she neglects the housework. You are the one who calls work to say she is sick. As the son of a drinking mother, you are expected to be your mother's companion and to take over the responsibilities of the man of the house. She may demand that you stay home with her rather than do things with your friends.

For both boys and girls, the embarrassment of drunken behavior by a mother is especially great because women who drink too much are more unacceptable to society than men who drink too much. A mother's drinking can be a much heavier burden for you to carry. It may also be harder for you to understand. Mothers are supposed to be nurturing, to take care of their children, to put the needs of their family first, and you cannot understand why your mother is not doing what she is supposed to. Her disease is no different from the disease in a man. She cannot stop drinking; she cannot stop the way she is behaving; she cannot help what the disease is doing to her. It is not her fault that she has the disease.

With some young people it is so obvious that a parent drinks too much that denial is no big deal. For most, however, the realization that a parent is having problems because of drinking too much is a shattering experience. When they admit to themselves that their parent may be an alcoholic, the foundation of their world crumbles just as Joan's did. Feelings of helplessness and hopelessness may take over. It seems as though there is nothing they can do to help the situation. Having some idea of what to do and what not to do can help overcome the feelings of hopelessness.

WHAT NOT TO DO

Do not take things personally. When the yelling and name-calling and putdowns are flying, it is difficult to keep from feeling hurt. At those times tell yourself that your parent has a disease. It is the bottle talking, not your parent. When your sober parent does the same thing, remember that she is suffering from the same disease, and the stress is causing her to strike out. Try to forgive your parents for things that seem thoughtless or uncaring. They both feel guilty, angry, lonely, unloved, and unlovable, and they are dealing with those feelings in the only way they know how. Unfortunately, their way is to project those terrible feelings onto you. Your part of the disease is to take those things very personally rather than recognizing them as alcoholism talking.

Do not overreact. You may find yourself becoming very sensitive with other people. You may be offended by something that was not meant to offend at all. When the teacher says he is tired of people who do not do their homework, and you are upset because he is criticizing you when you do have your homework done, you have taken personally something that was not meant for you; you have overreacted. When a friend says, "Boy, you sure get mad over nothing lately," you have probably been overreacting to things that were not meant in a personal way. Take a look at what you are getting upset about, and see if you may be overreacting. If a friend compliments someone else and you feel neglected or put down, it is more than likely overreaction on your part. Because you get so little nurturing at home and the atmosphere is so negative, you read negative into innocent things. Your need for support is so great that you tend to see only the lack of support that is so much a part of your life. Instead of taking things personally and overreacting, give people the benefit of the doubt and take things in a positive way.

Do not blame. That goes for blaming yourself as well as other people and things. You are not to blame for your parent's drinking, for the conflict between your parents, for your brother's being in trouble, for the dog's unhappiness because your sister did not feed him, for the teacher's distress that the class will not cooperate, for your father's anger that it is raining and he cannot go fishing, for your mother's anger because she is frustrated, for your friend's sadness, for your cat's running away. When you live in an alcoholic home, you sometimes think you are to blame for everything that goes wrong in the world. You have no more to do with causing your parent to drink than you do with causing the rain. Do not blame your parent for his drinking either. He already feels terrible about himself and adding more guilt will cause him to become defensive and reinforce his denial. Avoid comments like, "If you really cared about us you would come home on time," or "Everyone else's mother was at the Mother-Daughter Tea," or "You made me feel so bad when you yelled at my friends and told them to leave. They'll never speak to me again, and it's all your fault!" or "You promised not to drink last night, and you got drunk anyway." Making your parent feel more guilty and bad about himself will not cause him to seek help. In fact, such comments will cause him to feel sorry for himself because no one understands and everyone is on his case, and it gives him a good excuse to drink more!

Do not ride with your parent when he has been drinking if you can possibly avoid it. If both parents are with you, ask your drinking parent to let your other parent drive home. If you have a driver's license, ask your parent to let you drive. When other people are with you, ask one of the other adults to offer to drive your family home. You may have to tell your parent, "I'm afraid to ride in the car with you driving because you have been drinking." He may tell you that he is not drunk. In that case stick to your original statement and say, "I'm afraid to ride with you driving because you've been drinking." Do not get into a discussion about whether he is drunk or not. Simply say that he has been drinking. Sometimes you have no choice because your parent threatens you or forces you into the car, but if you do have a choice, take a bus or taxi, call a friend or relative. You may be able to plan what you will do as a family if you talk with your sober parent beforehand. Your drinking parent may be very angry, but *you will stay alive.*

Do not try to control the drinking; it is not possible. Hiding bottles, emptying bottles, looking for hidden bottles and throwing them away are futile and cause your drinking parent to spend money your family needs for other things to replace his supply. Do not bother demanding promises not to drink because the drinker cannot keep the promises. Counting drinks and trying to divert his attention to other things when you think he has had enough will not work either. Watering down the liquor and making weak drinks will make him angry. The drinking is uncontrollable until the drinker gets help.

Do not rescue and cover up. When your parent passes out on the living room floor, let him find himself there when he wakes up in the morning. Allow him to find his car parked in the neighbor's rosebushes in the morning. Better yet, let the neighbor tell him to get his car out of the rosebushes! Families often worry about what the neighbors might think if they found out. There is no need to worry about the neighbors finding out; *they know already.* The only ones who think it is a secret are in your family. By calling the boss to say the drinker is sick, putting him to bed when he passes out on the floor, or parking the car where it belongs, you are rescuing the drinker from the negative consequences of his behavior and you are enabling him to continue drinking without having to deal with the effects of the drinking. You do this with the best of intentions and the worst of results. It is only through facing the consequences of his behavior that the drinker can come to realize that his drinking is interfering with his life. The pain from the results of the drinking must be greater than the pain he is trying to escape in order for him to seek help.

Do not isolate yourself from others. As things get worse and worse at home, you may find you are withdrawing and isolating yourself. Your room may be the only place where you feel comfortable. Perhaps you feel your friends do not understand, and you may be afraid to bring anyone home because your parent is so unpredictable. You feel that friends will not like you if they find out what goes on at your house. Friends will not blame you for your parent's behavior. You need to be with other people. Your friends know that your parent drinks too much. Explain that your parent has a disease and talk about it. If you cannot talk about it, talk about other things. There are lots of things to share with friends, and it will help you get your mind on more pleasant things than the chaos at home. You need to be with other people.

WHAT TO DO

Go to Alateen. The support you will find there will help you weather the storms of living with an alcoholic. Look in the phone book under Al-Anon, and be sure to say you want to know about Alateen.

Break the No-Talk Rule. You may have a friend you can talk to, and that is good. However, it is very important that you get involved with an adult. If there is a counselor in your school who knows about chemical dependency, that is a good person to start with. If there is no special chemical dependency counselor, look for a counselor you feel comfortable with or a teacher or a nurse you can talk to. If there are no adults at school whom you feel you can trust, perhaps a minister or a priest could help you. Look in the phone book under alcoholism and drug abuse. If your school has a chapter of SADD (Students Against Driving Drunk), the adviser might be someone to confide in. Your health teacher might be able to give you some ideas of places and people who could help you. It is very important to look for adult help.

Talk to your sober parent. When the excuses for behavior come up, let your parent know that you know that the other parent was drinking. "Mom isn't sick, Dad, she's hung over." "The pressure at the office doesn't make Dad forget; he doesn't remember things he says when he's been drinking." It is very scary to say things like that. You will not know how your parent will react, and you will be afraid of making him or her angry. Take the chance; it is the only way to get your family to the help that is needed.

Always consider the physical safety of you and your family first. Have a plan like Joan's in case your parent should get violent. If you feel comfortable going to a neighbor's house, do that. If you are in danger and do not feel comfortable going to a neighbor's house, GO ANYWAY. Safety is the most important thing. In many areas you can dial 911 for any emergency. If you are not under that system, have a list of numbers to call in an emergency. Include a family member or friend who can come to your house if needed; the fire department in case your drinking parent sets the house on fire accidentally; the police in case of violence; a local children's shelter in case you need a place to stay and have no family member or neighbor to stay with; your doctor and an ambulance service in case your parent falls and hurts himself or something else happens requiring medical attention. Make two lists so you can carry one with you and leave one at home in a safe, convenient place.

Let your parent who drinks too much know that you love and care about him. Do that when he has not been drinking, and do it often. A very difficult thing to do, but very worthwhile, is to simply say, "I'm really worried about your drinking." If your parent snarls at you and tells you to mind your own business, do not say anything. If you must reply to what is said, say very calmly, "I just wanted you to know how worried I am because I love you." Because of his feelings of self-hate, your parent needs to know that you care and needs to hear you say it.

Have interests outside your home. Consider getting involved in activities or a club at school. Take up a hobby; start running or weight training; do volunteer work at a day-care center or with senior citizens; organize a SADD group at your school; get involved in church activities; join the choir at school or at church. It is important that you get the focus off of what is going on with the alcoholic and onto what is going on with you. Get your mind off what is wrong and onto what is right—and you and your welfare are what is right!

Learn all you can about alcoholism. Your Alateen group will announce speakers who are going to talk about alcoholism. Go

to those meetings. Read the literature provided at Al-Anon and
Alateen meetings. Get some literature from Alcoholics Anonymous and your local Council on Alcoholism. Look in the library
for other books about drugs and alcohol. Take an active part in
your school's drug education programs. The more you know
about the disease of alcoholism, the more you will understand
yourself and your family.

*Leave some of your AA, Al-Anon, and Alateen literature
around the house.* Your parents might read it, or it might be
thrown away. You never can tell what will happen. It may get
your sober parent to Al-Anon. Your parent who drinks may
even read it, and although nothing may happen immediately, it
may have an effect later on.

Finally, stop worrying and start taking care of yourself. Begin
to see things in terms of what you *can* do, and do them. Work on
getting the most out of life for you. Looking at your situation as
hopeless and out of your control puts you in the pits. It is time to
grab the rope along the wall of the pit and pull yourself out.
Millions of young people are living in the same chaos you are.
Sitting around feeling sorry for yourself will not change anything. If the world looks bad to you and you think you cannot
change the world, you are right. The only thing you can change
is the way *you* look at the world, and there are people in your
world who can help you learn to look at things in a more positive way. The choice is yours.

CHAPTER V

Intervention

Carol Swig sat staring at her daughter Joan in disbelief. She wanted to cover her ears and run screaming out of the room, but she was rooted to her chair. She did not want to hear what Joan was saying, yet she could do nothing to stop the words that were spilling out of Joan's mouth. Joan was saying out loud what Carol had feared for so long, and Carol did not know whether to be angry or relieved that Joan had talked to an alcoholism counselor. When Joan asked her to go with her to see the counselor, Carol did not answer, and Joan burst into tears. Seeing Joan cry was more than Carol could handle, and when she put her arms around Joan to comfort her, Carol began to cry as well. They sat holding each other and crying until Joan asked again if Carol would see Melanie, and her mother agreed.

Once the No-Talk Rule was broken, Joan could not stop talking. For over two hours she shared her feelings and what she had learned with her mother. Joan felt good about being able to answer some of her mother's questions, and she especially felt good about having the subject of her father's drinking out in the open.

The following day Carol and Joan met with Melanie and learned about intervention, a process for helping alcoholics and addicts get the help they need to interrupt their destructive use of chemicals. Carol was overwhelmed because she knew so little about alcoholism; she had not known that it was a treatable disease and that there were treatment facilities right in town. What she had learned about alcoholism from Joan had helped her a great deal, and having her questions answered by Melanie made it a little better for her. Carol's greatest fear had been that she might be expected to confront Jim herself. Melanie assured her that she would have a support team and would not have to do anything by herself; in fact, confronting Jim by herself would be the worst thing she could do. The intervention would be well

59

planned, and they would have much work to do before they approached Jim.

Because she knew the fear and confusion that Carol and Joan were feeling, Melanie gave them a general idea of what intervention is all about. She explained that it used to be thought that no one could help an alcoholic until he wanted to be helped; however, through the process of intervention, a person can be presented with the realities of the destruction his chemical use is causing and can be convinced that he must seek treatment for his disease.

Joan wanted to know how she and her mother could possibly make her father see reality when he would not listen to anyone. Agreeing that they probably could not accomplish that by themselves, Melanie said that was why an intervention team was so important. The team would be made up of people who were important to her father—family members, friends, co-workers, people who cared about him, people he cared about and respected, people whose opinions were important to him. Joan did not think her father cared how she felt about him, but Melanie assured her that how his children felt about him was extremely important to any man even when he seemed not to care.

Melanie went on to say that once the team was chosen, they would have to meet several times to prepare for the intervention. The preparation was vitally important to the outcome. In answer to Carol's question about the preparation, Melanie said that she would meet with the team and give them some general background about alcoholism and intervention. Then there would be the gathering of information they would present at the intervention. Team members would have to share their information with the group and would have to rehearse how it would be presented. They would probably have to meet four or five times.

First they needed to choose their intervention team of people close to Jim who had been affected by his behavior while he was drinking. Besides family members, they needed to consider friends and people at work who were important to him. Melanie stressed that team members must not be alcohol or drug abusers themselves, or Jim would immediately discredit everything that was said.

After some discussion, in addition to the other children in the family, Danny, Robin, and Rick, it was decided to include Jim's brother Jay, because they were still very close and more than once Jay had told Jim to go easy on the drinking at family gatherings. Since Jim's job was very important to him and Carol knew that he had been warned about his long lunches and his work not being done on time, they decided to ask Jim's boss to be a part of the team. Almost all of Jim's friends were drinking buddies, but he did have one old friend, Dave, who had kept in touch and had been with him more than once when he had been drinking and had been embarrassed by Jim's behavior. Dave had confided to Carol that he hated to see Jim drinking so much and did not contact him more often because of it. Melanie encouraged Carol to call and ask Dave to be part of the team. Those three people plus Jim's four children and his wife would be a powerful intervention team, she was sure.

Since Joan had been the one to start the process and had done so much already, Carol asked her to help in talking to the other children. She also wanted Joan to be there when she talked to Jim's brother. Melanie agreed that Carol and Joan would be a good support team in talking to the family. It was decided that Carol would contact Steve, Jim's boss, and if she needed support she would ask Jay to go with her. Dave was someone Carol felt comfortable with, so she decided to see him on her own.

Before Carol and Joan left, they practiced what they would say to everyone. To be clear about their goal, Melanie had them write down what they wanted to accomplish when they talked to the prospective team members. They wrote that their goal was to get others to support them in confronting Jim with the destructiveness of his drinking so that he would be willing to go to treatment for his alcoholism. The first step was to get the others to come to see Melanie and become part of the intervention team. They worked on how they would approach each team member and decided to talk to Danny, Robin, and Rick together. Although she was still scared, by the time they were ready to leave Carol felt that she could handle things okay, and she and Joan felt closer than they had in a long time. As they were walking toward the door, Melanie suggested some books and pamphlets for Carol to read and recommended that she attend the Al-Anon meeting that was on the same night as the Alateen meeting that Joan attended. That Joan was going to Alateen was another surprise to Carol, but by now she was able to take surprise as a part of her day. She told Melanie she would think about going to Al-Anon.

Talking to Robin, Rick, and Danny was not as difficult as Carol had expected. They were relieved to have the "secret" out in the open. Rick was a little reluctant to take part in the intervention, but Carol told him that he only had to go to the first meeting. After that he could decide whether he wanted to continue. Having seen how she worked, Carol was sure that Melanie would gain Rick's cooperation if he went to the first meeting. He was not happy, but he agreed to go.

When Carol and Joan went to see Jim's brother Jay, Carol was stunned to find out that he had been considering calling her to discuss planning an intervention ever since Joan had asked him if she could call him if things got bad at home. Carol had not known about Joan's call to Jay and was embarrassed that he knew about Jim's violence. Joan apologized to her mother for not telling her, but when she had called her uncle she had not been able to tell her mother about it; and now it had slipped her mind with all that was going on. Before Joan knew what was happening, Jay told Carol that he was grateful that Joan had called him, and he was glad they were working together to do something about Jim's drinking. When Carol asked Jay to go with her to see Jim's boss, he agreed immediately.

On the way home from Jay's, Carol told Joan that she felt as though a huge weight had been lifted from her shoulders. It was good to know that she was not alone and others were there to help. In fact, she would even go to Al-Anon; she was willing to try anything that would make things easier to deal with.

Two days later Carol and Jay were in Steve's office asking him to be a member of the intervention team. Jim had worked for Steve for over ten years, and Steve was genuinely concerned about the way his drinking was interfering with his job performance. It was only because of their long association and friendship that Steve had not fired him. If being part of an intervention would help Jim, Steve was willing to give it a try.

With the cooperation of Jay and Steve, Carol did not feel so worried about approaching Dave and asking him to join the intervention team. His reaction was the same as the other two men, and Carol wasted no time in setting up an appointment for the team to meet with Melanie.

Since understanding the disease concept of alcoholism is so important, most of the first meeting of the intervention team was spent discussing alcoholism and the intervention process. For the next meeting they were each asked to make a list of specific incidents that they had seen or been involved with that related directly to Jim's drinking. They were told to be as detailed as possible. "You drink too much" was far too general. A specific, detailed example would be, "On my birthday you had a lot to drink and went over to Cindy and said she was beautiful and tried to kiss her. She was really embarrassed and I felt humiliated." Danny said he was not sure he could do it, but Joan and Robin said they would help him write things down and Rick offered to help him remember things that had happened. As her children were offering to work together, Carol had a feeling of wonder because it had been so long since they had done anything cooperatively. She left the meeting with a feeling of hope.

The second meeting of the intervention team was spend sharing lists, giving feedback, and revising lists. All of the secrets were out, and everyone was amazed at how much had been going on that they did not know about. They were also amazed at how many of their "secrets" were not so secret after all. Jay told Carol that if he had known things were so bad, he would have done something long ago. When the family had been making their lists, Carol was astonished to find out that things she thought she had kept hidden were common knowledge to the children. By the time all the lists were shared, there was a feeling of purpose and togetherness in the group. They all felt that they were doing the right thing.

The third meeting was a rehearsal. Melanie pretended to be Jim, and team members read their lists out loud one at a time. As they read, Melanie would interrupt and defend and justify the behavior they were describing. Sometimes members of the team would give their opinions of what Jim's reaction might be. They helped each other to think of ways they could respond to any outbursts of Jim's. When they had finished rehearsing their lists, Melanie suggested that they decide on some of the details of the intervention.

A most important thing was how they would end after the reading of the lists. They each had to take a stand that would motivate Jim to get treatment. For example, Steve could say that if Jim did not go for treatment he would be fired; however, Steve had to be prepared to follow through and not back down. No one could make a threat that they did not fully intend to keep if Jim refused treatment and kept drinking. If Carol said she would no longer live this way, she had to be prepared to move out and convince Jim that she meant it. If the children chose to back their mother, they had to be ready to move also. Whatever their stands were, Jim had to believe that they would not back down. The team decided to work on their stands and come back again for a final rehearsal.

On the day of the last rehearsal, the team carefully chose the order in which they would read their lists. They decided to have Steve begin because Jim's job was important to him and he had a lot of respect for Steve. Next would be Dave, then Jay, and finally, since they had definitely decided that they would not live with Jim's alcoholism any longer, Carol and the children. Joan would be last because she and Jim had had a special closeness before his alcoholism had become so bad.

The final details were where and when the intervention would be held and how they would get Jim there. Steve suggested that they have it early in the day in his office when Jim was most likely to be sober. He would just schedule a meeting with Jim as though it were an ordinary matter. They agreed to have the intervention the following week, so that Carol would have time to arrange for Jim to enter a treatment center on the day of the intervention. She would have to have the arrangements made and his bag packed and in the car, or he might try to avoid going by saying he did not know where to go. Also, he might agree and then back down later while arrangements were being made.

Once the details were taken care of, they went ahead with the rehearsal. It was a difficult experience even though they knew what to expect from each other. Just doing it without interruption for feedback or other conversation seemed to make it more serious than it had been before. They realized that the intervention was going to be difficult, but they were ready to go for it. Having Melanie's support and expertise gave them what they needed to carry on.

On the day of the intervention they all gathered in Steve's office fifteen minutes before the time set. Steve made sure that Jim would be involved in something that would keep him away from the office area where he might see the group come in. When he walked into the office, Jim was startled to see Jay, Dave, and his family. He immediately knew something was up, and he did not like it. The only stranger in the room was Melanie, and he definitely did not like her. Jay was the first one to speak; he said that they were all there because they cared about him. He introduced Melanie as a counselor they had all been working with because of their concern for him. Melanie took over from there, saying that this would be difficult for all of them, but his family and friends had some things that they needed to share with him. They wanted him to help them by listening. They knew it would be hard for him, but they needed to have him listen. Would he just listen for a while?

Jim growled that he would listen, but that was all. As Steve began to read his list Jim became more and more alarmed. He started to break in, but Melanie gently reminded him that he had agreed to listen. By the time Steve had finished, Jim could not speak. When Dave read his list, Jim looked uncomfortable and then as if he wanted to get angry. He grumbled something about what kind of a friend was it who never came to see you. Dave said that he missed being with Jim, but that the last time they had gone fishing Jim drank too much and called the captain of the fishing boat an idiot among other less complimentary things. The embarrassment was more than Dave wanted to go through again. Jim slid down in his chair and stared at the floor.

As Jay went through his list, Jim tried to look steely-eyed and uncaring until Jay said, "I love you a lot; you've always been my favorite brother, but last Christmas when you stood out on my front lawn, so drunk you couldn't stand without swaying, and yelled that you didn't give a damn if I thought you drank too much, I was ashamed you were my brother." Jay's voice broke, and Jim put his head in his hands and said, "I'm so sorry."

As Carol and the children read their lists, Jim tried to look unconcerned and unaffected, but his comments were less and less forceful until he had stopped talking and was just listening. By the time Joan read her list, Jim looked as though he had given up. One by one the members of the team told Jim the stands they had taken concerning his drinking and urged him to get help. When he said he did not know where to get help, Carol told him that she had made arrangements for him to go to a treatment center right here in town. When he found out that the stay in treatment was twenty-eight days, he began to protest that he could not take a month off work to go anywhere, but Steve told him that the company insurance would pay the bill for treatment and his job would be waiting for him when he got back. If he chose not to go to treatment, he could consider himself unemployed from that minute on. Jim was stunned and started to protest until he looked at Steve's eyes. When he said he would go first thing in the morning, Jay told him that Carol had packed a bag for him and that the three of them could check him in at the treatment center while Dave took the kids home. At that point all of his resistance melted, and he went out with Carol and Jay.

As Melanie looked at the people left in the room, she saw relief, concern, sorrow, exhaustion, triumph, and apprehension all mixed together on their faces. She sighed and thought to herself that another family had taken the first small step toward recovery.

MORE ABOUT INTERVENTION

The intervention for Jim Swig illustrates how the process works. You can begin the process in your family the same way Joan Swig did in hers. You may not have someone come to you as Melanie Mender did by speaking to Joan's health class, but you can find someone qualified to help you by calling your local National Council on Alcoholism. The NCA can give you a referral for alcoholism intervention, and most of the specialists on their referral lists are also qualified drug abuse counselors as well.

If you do not have an NCA branch in your city, look in the yellow pages of your phone book under Alcoholism and Drug Abuse. Call and talk to someone. There are three important questions you need to have answered. Does the person or treatment facility believe in the disease concept of chemical dependency? Does the person support the intervention process? Has the person participated in interventions? If you get "yes" answers to all three questions, you can probably get competent help from the counselor or treatment facility.

Your community has what you need, and all you need do is ask. It is important to have qualified, experienced help in your intervention, because a chemically dependent person will reinforce his defense system and be even harder to reach if the intervention attempt is not done correctly.

Intervention, properly planned, almost always works. It was the careful planning and hard work by the intervention team that made it possible for Jim Swig to see the destructive effects of his drinking at home, in his community, and at work. He saw how he was hurting himself and others. The consequences of his continued drinking became so painful that he had to stop. He did not have to lose everything, hit bottom, and ask for help on his own. His family and friends provided a bottom for him and showed him the way to get help.

Although intervention worked with Jim, it does not work with everyone. What if it does not work in your family? Then you must try again. Sometimes the planning phase of the intervention is not adequate and the process breaks down. Sometimes the dependent person's denial is not broken. Do not give up. The intervention will spoil his drinking from that time on. That is why a second or even a third intervention can be worthwhile, so get help and plan another intervention. Continue with your own recovery by going to Alateen or Al-Anon and getting off the merry-go-round of chemical dependency. You need support to do that, but once your family has participated in an intervention, you will have conquered your helplessness and can support each other and get help from others in your Al-Anon and Alateen groups. You can continue your own counseling and stay in recovery for your co-dependency.

A WORD ABOUT TREATMENT

A variety of chemical dependency treatment programs are available. Some are inpatient programs and some are outpatient. Inpatient programs require the dependent person to go into a hospital or treatment facility for a period of time; the average length of stay is twenty-eight days. Most treatment providers recognize addiction as a family disease and have active family programs. Aftercare is also a vital part of a treatment and recovery plan, and attendance at Alcoholics Anonymous, Al-Anon, Alateen, Narcotics Anonymous, or other support groups is part of the program.

Outpatient programs can be very effective. They do not require dependents to leave home, but to see a counselor on a regular basis and often participate in group therapy as well. A good outpatient program includes the family, recognizing that the co-dependency of family members needs treating also. It is important that outpatient counselors consider chemical dependency a primary disease and not a symptom of some underlying emotional problem.

If outpatient care is not enough support for the dependent, the counselor refers the client to inpatient treatment. When looking for a treatment center, ask for brochures that describe the program. Some questions you may want to have answered are: Does the program include the family? (A strong family program is important to the recovery of the chemically dependent person as well as being vital to the well-being and recovery of the family.) What kind of aftercare is provided? (If it is only for a few weeks, it is not enough support.) Does the family have an aftercare program? What kind of community support do they recommend? (They should recommend A.A., Al-Anon, Alateen, and Narcotics Anonymous.) Do they believe in intervention? (Some do not, and you will not get the help you need to do a needed intervention.)

Treatment is only the first step on the road to recovery. Going through a treatment program does not mean that a person is "cured"; chemical dependency is a chronic disease and can only be arrested. Relapse is not unusual. Chemically dependent people and their families must always consider themselves *recovering*, so that they do not slip into a sense of complacency and carelessness. The disease of chemical dependency is powerful and subtle; it waits for you to let your guard down and then attacks in greater fury than ever. Alcoholics Anonymous meetings are full of stories of people with ten, fifteen, and even twenty-five years of sobriety who returned to drinking. Many regain sobriety, but some die as a result of their dependency. Families who thought they had nothing to worry about can be thrown back into the helplessness and hopelessness that the disease of chemical dependency thrives on.

Continuing in a program of recovery is an important part of the life of a chemically dependent family, for recovery is a process, not an event. Intervention is the first step in that process. You are never recovered but always recovering, and your life can get better and better as time goes on.

CHAPTER VI

Chemically Dependent Teens

The judge had said that he could go to juvenile hall for a year or to a drug treatment program, and Dean Nile did not like either choice. The burglary charge was a bum rap in the first place, and he did not have a drug problem in the second place. The whole thing was stupid, and the judge was the most stupid thing of all, yet here he was, in the car with his parents going to a stupid drug treatment place that was going to be just as bad as the hall. The only good thing was that it would not be a year long; not if he had anything to do about it anyway. Dean was angry, but that was nothing new. He had been angry for a long time. What he did not want to admit was that he was scared. The last year had been a nightmare, and he had thought he would never wake up. Now he felt as though he were plunged even more deeply into the terror in his mind. Where were they taking him, and what was going to be done to him there? How had this happened to him? How could things have gotten so messed up?

Dean's story is typical of thousands of young people who started out having fun and ended up in despair. His first experience with any kind of drug was taking sips of his dad's beer when he was a little kid. When Dean was ten, he was at the park and some older boys were smoking pot. They asked him if he wanted to get high. Dean was a little afraid of marijuana, but he was more afraid of what the older boys would think of him if he said no, so he smoked pot for the first time. It was really no big deal because he did not have very much, and he did not know what it was supposed to feel like. It did make him feel grown up and gave him the thrill that comes with doing something he knew his parents would not approve of. A few months later the boys did give him enough to get high, and Dean really liked the feeling. From that time until he got into junior high, Dean smoked pot once in a while when it was around, but he did not go looking for it; and he drank some of his dad's beer or bourbon and gingerale when his dad was involved in a TV program and would not notice.

When Dean got into junior high, it was sort of scary being in such a big school, and he felt pretty much alone because he had no close friends there. Some of the older boys who hung around the park were there, and they remembered Dean and were friendly to him. They asked him if he wanted to smoke a little weed, and before he knew it he was late for his first-period math class two or three mornings a week because he was getting high before school. When the first-quarter grades came out, Dean had a C in math, and he had always had As before. His parents were very angry and restricted him after school until his math grade improved.

Dean was angry about the restriction; he was sure that his math teacher had given him the bad grade because she did not like him. When his mother called Ms. Numero about the grade, she made a big deal out of the time or two he had been late to class.

Basketball season started, and Dean went out for the team. He had been a good player in sixth grade, so he was looking forward to being on the team. He was still getting high with his friends before school most mornings, and now he was also meeting them at lunch and getting high. Sometimes he was late to English after lunch or fell asleep in class. Then he began to cut English once or twice a week. He always made it to basketball practice, but since he was still half high, his performance on the court was not very good, and he was not chosen for the first string. Dean decided that the coach did not choose him for the starting lineup because he did not like him. That made him angry, and he quit the team.

By spring, Dean was spending every possible minute with his using friends. He would see them before his last-period class and they would decide to cut last period and go get high. Dean's grades were a mess compared to the As and Bs he always had before. By the final report at the end of the school year, Dean had Ds in three subjects and Cs in four.

Also by the end of the school year things were a mess at home. His parents were always on his case about school, and they were giving him fits about doing stuff around the house. They made a big deal about his messy room and were always nagging him to take out the garbage, put his dirty dishes in the dishwasher, mow the lawn, feed the dog, or do some other piddly thing. They were just looking for excuses to bug him. If he came in late for dinner, you would think he had committed a major crime. Dean could hardly wait for summer.

The summer between seventh and eighth grade was a real blast for Dean. He met his buddies every day to mellow out. They bought weed when they had money and stole beer or liquor when they did not. They did a little shoplifting so they could trade for weed. After being with his friends all day, Dean went home and right to his room and cranked up his radio. His parents complained that he never did anything with the family anymore, but he did not want to be bothered with them. Sometimes he woke up at two or three in the morning so hungry he could not believe it. If there were nothing he wanted to eat in the house, he went out his window and down to the all-night convenience store to buy something. Sometimes he called his friend Stewart and met Stew someplace for a few hours. Dean always made sure that he was in the house before his parents got up. His mother complained because he slept until noon, but he told her it was summer so he did not have to get up any earlier. If she gave him too bad a time, he got mad and stomped out.

Dean could not remember too much about eighth grade because he was high so much of the time, but he did manage to keep from failing anything, getting Ds in all subjects. He got in trouble for truancy and was suspended several times for disruptive behavior—calling teachers names, refusing to obey teachers' requests—and for possession of marijuana. He told his parents that he was holding the marijuana for someone else, that he did not use it himself, and they believed him. When he was suspended for being under the influence, he said it was the first time he had ever gotten high and he would never do it again. The school made such a fuss about it that his parents decided to take Dean to a counselor.

Going to the counselor was a real joke. Dean lied about his drug use and told the counselor that everything would be fine if his parents were not so messed up. He complained that they did not want to let him do anything or go anywhere and that they were the reason for his anger and defiance at school. The counselor told the Niles that Dean was just exhibiting normal teenage rebellion and that they needed to give him more opportunity to make decisions for himself and to allow him more freedom. That ended the sessions with the counselor, and Dean felt justified in his treatment of his parents and in his behavior.

His parents, in Dean's opinion, were still a real pain in the rear, and he stayed away from home as much as possible. On weekends he was out until two or three o'clock in the morning. It was "party hardy" all weekend. Some mornings Dean could not remember what happened at the party or how he got home. His friends would tell him what a great time he had the night before. Dean did not know that he was experiencing alcoholic blackouts.

During this time, Dean and his friends began using a wider variety of drugs. Marijuana was never refused, but they had added LSD, PCP, hashish, and amphetamines (speed, mostly in pill form, but they would snort sometimes too.) Buying drugs was getting expensive, so Dean had to steal more to support his habit. Since the family silver was used only on holidays, Dean took a few pieces to trade for drugs. When his parents' friends came over and left coats and purses in the guest room, he took money out of wallets and pockets. Sneaking into his parents' room and taking money out of his father's wallet and his mother's purse was a regular occurrence.

When Dean's parents accused him of stealing, he got angry and denied taking anything. He accused them of blaming him for everything that went wrong in the house and told them they were unfair. Shouting obscenities and blaming them for causing his problems, he would storm out, saying that even the counselor knew they were terrible parents and he could not stand living there. He began staying out all night and occasionally was gone from Friday to Sunday.

Within a month of entering ninth grade, Dean was transferred to a continuation high school because of his truancy. Some days he went to school and some days he did not. When he did go to school, he did not always make it to all classes. School was just not important, and Dean did not care whether he graduated or not. He just wanted to get high and stay high. It took more and more weed or speed to get high, and he could drink a six-pack without feeling the way he wanted to feel. Dean's tolerance for drugs and alcohol had built up so much that to get high and stay high he needed more money. He could no longer steal from his parents because they were not leaving wallets and purses around anymore. The silver was locked up, as was his mother's jewelry. So Dean began "doing houses" with his friends and dealing pot and acid as well. He had begun using cocaine when he could get it, but it was so expensive that he usually settled for crystal meth.

The first time Dean was arrested for burglary, his parents went down to juvenile hall and brought him home. They hired a lawyer, and when the judge gave them a choice they agreed to pay restitution so that Dean would not have to spend time in juvenile hall. Dean showed his appreciation by going out with his friends and coming home drunk and throwing up all over the living room rug.

Dean did not care how his parents felt or what they thought; he just wanted to get high, and he did not care whether they knew it or not. He had long since quit going to school, and when his parents said anything about school or objected to his behavior, he shouted obscenities at them and called them names. When his father grabbed him to stop him from leaving one day, Dean hit him, and they ended up rolling on the floor. He did not come home for four days.

As time went on, whenever Dean got into a fight with his parents he disappeared for days, going from one friend's house to another or sleeping outside when the weather was good. Dean was tired of the way his parents treated him. Actually, he was tired of everything, and the only way he could get any energy was to get loaded on speed. When he was wired, he could go for days without eating or sleeping. He was thin, and his eyes looked sunk in his skull. He had a constant cough, could not seem to remember things, and was having flashbacks. He felt lonely and unloved, and even though he tried to cover it up by staying high, Dean felt guilty and hated himself. Sometimes he thought he would be better off if he was dead.

When Dean and his buddies were caught in a house, arrested, and charged with forty-two counts of burglary, he blamed it all on the nosy old lady who saw them from her window and called the police. He could not believe it when his parents told the judge that he was out of control because he had a drug problem. As far as Dean was concerned, he did not have a drug problem, and the only ones with a problem were his parents. If they would just leave him alone, everything would be fine, in his opinion. And now because of a nosy old biddy, parents who just wanted to get rid of him, and a stupid judge, he was going to a drug treatment program. His life was totally messed up!

Entering the treatment center the same day as Dean Nile was Connie Vivial. Connie's drug using began much the same way as Dean's. When she was very small, she would drink the last few drops of beer in the cans that were left sitting around, or when her parents had friends over, she would empty the glasses left around the house. Her parents and their friends would laugh at Connie and say she was a chip off the old block, just like her dad. By the time Connie was eight, she was fixing drinks for her dad so he did not have to get up and do it himself. She would fix one for herself while she was at it.

School was okay as far as Connie was concerned, but she did not do particularly well, getting Cs most of the time with a B now and then. When she began junior high, it was really scary. None of her friends were in her classes, and they seemed to make friends with new people very easily. Connie was very lonely during seventh grade. She was still drinking at home a lot of the time because it made her feel better about being so lonely.

When Connie started eighth grade, she met Merry Maiker. Merry had lots of friends who liked to have fun, and they invited Connie to a party. Connie was flattered that such a lively group would notice her, and her parents were happy to see Connie getting more involved with others her own age. The night of the party Connie stayed at Merry's. The Vivials did not know that Merry's parents would not be home, nor did they know that the party was at the home of an older friend of Merry's whose parents were away. The party was a "kegger," and the purpose was to get drunk—to drink until the booze was gone or until you passed out, whichever came first. There was lots of marijuana at the party and other drugs too. Connie got high on pot for the first time and loved it. She also got drunk, but that was not new to her. She was not sure how she got back to Merry's house or what happened at the party after about eleven-thirty, but Merry said that they had both had a wonderful time and two boys had brought them home. The boys were going to come by that afternoon. Connie was supposed to be home by noon, but she called her parents and told them that Merry's parents had asked her to stay and go to a movie with them that afternoon. That began what was to be Connie's long career of lies and deceit.

The boys, who were sixteen, did come over that afternoon, and Connie was thrilled that older boys would be interested in a thirteen-year-old. Party time had begun for Connie Vivial. It meant that her homework did not get done because she was too busy figuring out ways to get out of the house and meet boys. When she was in class, all she could think about was boys. She was not getting her chores done at home because she was too preoccupied, and she spent every weekend partying. Her parents wanted her home by eleven-thirty, so Connie tried to spend as many weekends as possible with friends. Her parents were not sure that all of this staying with friends was good, especially since they did not know any of the parents of Connie's friends.

When Connie got her report card with all Ds and unsatisfactory-effort grades, she hid it from her parents. She was supposed to return it signed to school, and when her home-room teacher asked for it, Connie kept saying she forgot it. Finally, after two weeks, her teacher mailed a copy of the report card to her home. When Connie got home from school, her mother, furious, was waiting for her. Of course, Connie had to go through a scene with her mother and then another when her father got home. When the smoke of battle cleared, Connie had been restricted and was forbidden to go out on weekends.

There was no way Connie was going to stay in on weekends, so she would wait until her parents were asleep and sneak out her bedroom window. Since she was hanging around older boys, more drugs were available to her. She was dropping acid on a regular basis and did cocaine when it was available. Since she was sneaking out on school nights as well as weekends, Connie always had pills to pep her up and keep her going during the day. She was cutting school, and by the end of the year she had failed two classes and was required to go to summer school.

Because she did not want to be left back, Connie did go to summer school and passed her classes. She was also partying at the lake as often as possible. Her parents thought she was going to the park to take recreational classes, but she was meeting her friends to party every day. Sex, drugs, and hard rock were where it was that summer. Home was where it was *not*. Her parents were doing everything they could to keep Connie from going out with her friends. They blamed Merry for Connie's bad attitude and refused to allow her in the house. Everything they did only made Connie angrier, and she refused to do anything around the house. When the fighting really got bad, Connie split and stayed away for a month.

While she was a runaway, Connie stayed with a boyfriend who was nineteen. He was working as a dishwasher and did not make much money, and since Connie had been shoplifting for quite a while to get money for drugs, she was able to add to his income by doing more selective shoplifting for a guy she knew. After a month she was tired of always having to scrounge for money for food and drugs, and her boyfriend wanted someone to help him pay the rent, so Connie decided to go home.

It was two weeks after school started when Connie returned home, and her parents insisted that she go to school. She was not interested in school, but she agreed to go just to get them off her back. She was really tired of their interference, but she did not want to leave right then. Most days Connie left home late for school and met her friends at the park a block from school. While they got high, they would decide what to do that day. Usually they hung around outside, but when the weather got cold, they went to someone's house whose parents were both working.

When her parents finally were notified that Connie was being transferred to a continuation high school for poor attendance, they went into orbit, blaming the school for not notifying them that Connie had been absent so much. Connie did not care what the school did or what her parents did, but when her parents jumped all over her and screamed and raged, she said, "Later," and left. This time there was no boyfriend to stay with, so Connie stayed with Patti Pardee. Patti's mother thought Connie's parents were horribly unfair and lacking in good communication with their daughter. She thought it was too bad they would not listen when Connie explained that she did not realize she would be marked absent when she had only been late if she did not sign in at the office. Mrs. Pardee had wanted to call Connie's parents to tell them where she was, but Connie said she was afraid that her father would do something terrible to her or to them if he found out where she was.

The Pardees kept Connie for two weeks before Mrs. Pardee realized that Connie really was not going to school and that Patti was not going either. They blamed Connie for Patti's truancy and told her that she had better go home. Having no intention of going home, Connie found another friend to help her out. She stayed in the toolshed at Sarah Sixtie's house, and Sarah let her in the house to eat and to shower after her parents left for work in the morning. Finally, after five weeks, Connie ran out of friends to help her, and she ended up sleeping in the park. She could get enough drugs to keep her going by exchanging sex for drugs with the boys who hung around the park, but she was hungry much of the time and was doing crank to ease the hunger. Feeling really burnt out and down on herself, Connie realized that doing drugs was no fun anymore but that she needed to use just to feel okay. To get high, to feel the way she used to when she first started using was what Connie was after, and it just would not come. If she did not use, she felt even worse. She did not know what to do, but she knew she could not stop using. She hated herself for not being able to stop and for doing the things she had to do to get drugs. Connie would close her eyes at night and wish she did not have to wake up.

Knowing that she had no other choice, looking like a scarecrow and feeling like crud, Connie went home. She walked in the house as though she had never been gone, said hello to her parents, and went toward her room. She was not surprised when her father stopped her, but she was surprised when he did not come unglued and start ranting and raving. Her surprise became complete amazement when both her parents said she could not stay at home until she quit using drugs, that she had to see a drug counselor before they would let her back in the house. Connie could not believe her ears. She had been sure that her parents did not know about her drug use, and here they were kicking her out of the house unless she saw a drug counselor.

The Vivials took Connie to a drug counselor for adolescents, who recommended that she enter an inpatient treatment program especially for adolescents. So here she was, entering the treatment center the same day as Dean Nile and a boy named Joe Jocque.

Joe Jocque was a clean-cut, muscular, athletic-looking seventeen-year-old. He looked self-confident and sure of himself. Glancing around at the other people in the reception room, Joe was sure that he would not be here very long. One look at the burnouts sitting there, and he knew he had nothing to worry about. Besides, his dad would get him out of this just as Dad got him out of everything else. He just wished he could smoke a joint to calm his nerves a little. The whole idea of his being here was ridiculous. His mother and those stupid friends of hers were responsible for it. They had no right to search his room, and then they made a big deal about finding a little coke. The whole thing was stupid, and his dad did not like it any better than he did. Joe was sure that when he talked to whoever he had to talk to, they would all find out how stupid they were and he would be out in no time. Everybody drank and used drugs. Joe did not use any more than anyone else he hung around with.

Joe's drinking started just like anyone else's. On holidays his parents let him drink wine with dinner. When he was very small, they mixed it half and half with water. When they were drinking and left glasses around, Joe took sips out of them. He especially liked the taste of whiskey. When he was in junior high, he and some of his teammates would get together and drink beer on Friday nights to celebrate if they had won the football game or to mourn if they had lost. If they did not meet on Friday, they would have a little party on Saturday. They would tell some of the girls where the party would be, and they would all have a good time.

By high school, drinking beer and smoking pot went with playing football and basketball; everybody used. Since Joe's family was well off, he always had money and could buy drugs whenever he wanted. During his freshman and sophomore years, he tried a lot of stuff—acid, PCP, uppers, downers, snorting speed and cocaine. He really liked cocaine and began dealing so he could assure himself a steady supply. Besides, it was pretty expensive, and he needed to deal or it would have cost him too much for himself.

School had always been a snap for Joe, and staying eligible was easy. He did not worry about getting As because he was such a good football player that he would be able to get into almost any college he chose. Joe's father had been an all-conference running back in college and was being looked at by the pros until a knee injury took him out of the lineup in his senior year. Knowing how important the game was to his father, Joe felt that he had to play well and not let him down. That was a lot of pressure, and Joe needed to take something to get himself up for the games. He usually took pills to get himself moving. When he had it, he would snort a few lines of coke, but it was easier to carry the pills. A lot of the guys on the team did the same thing.

For Joe's sixteenth birthday, his parents gave him a TransAm. He had it for only two months when he turned it over and totaled it going too fast on a curve. It was just an error in judgment, and according to Joe's dad, it was not unusual for a kid to make that kind of mistake. What Joe never told anyone was that he had snorted three lines of coke at his friend's house that night. When the insurance company paid off the claim, Joe asked his dad to replace the car with a Corvette. Cautioning him not to drive too fast, his dad had the Corvette in the driveway two days later.

Since Joe was driving and had a steady girlfriend, he mentioned how fast his money went for gas and dates. His dad agreed that it could really be expensive and raised his allowance. Joe did not mention that supplying coke for two was what was really expensive because Joe wanted to share the fantastic high with his girl.

Things were just great for Joe. Every once in a while his mother got on his case for being gone so much, but his father always defended him and said he was just being a kid. Most of the time Joe just ignored his mother. She got excited over nothing. During football season the first year Joe was in high school, his mother had a fit when she found Joe and his father drinking beer while they watched the Monday night football game on TV. You would have thought someone was being murdered. She would really have flipped if she had known that Joe could drink a six-pack on his own and not even feel much of a buzz. His father was proud that Joe was no lightweight with his beer drinking. An athlete had to be "one of the guys."

Drinking beer with the guys was great, but when Joe partied he always brought a fifth of Jack Daniels. J.D. and J.D. was his favorite drink. Give the Seven-Up to the girls; he wanted his booze clean and straight. Joe had a reputation for being able to hold his liquor and for having plenty of weed and coke, so he was always welcome at a party. After a party one night, Joe forgot that his parents had said they were going out and would be coming in late, and he got home before they had gone to bed. He was drunk, and his dad read the riot act to him about driving when he had been drinking. Since his dad had a hangover himself the next day, Joe wondered where he got off making such a big deal about somebody else drinking and driving.

Football season in senior year Joe was given the most valuable player trophy. He was flying high—in more ways than one. He was doing coke every day, and after football season he was smoking marijuana three or four times a day. His mother noticed the cough and runny nose that went along with that, and she began to question him about his health. She was really beginning to annoy him, which was not surprising since he was jumpy and irritable if he was not on something all the time. His mother complained about his attitude and smart mouth to his father, but Mr. Jocque was working sixty hours a week and saw very little of Joe, and he thought his wife was making something out of nothing as usual.

His mother really became a pain when she started going to Toughlove. Joe had noticed for several months that she was being hard on him about doing stuff around the house and getting home on time and that he had more trouble getting what he wanted from her, but he did not know that she was going to a Toughlove Parent Support Group until he came home one day and found a strange couple in the living room with her. The three of them had searched his room and found what he had stashed there, and they had the drugs, pipes, and some other stuff piled on the table. Joe tried to lie out of it, but the strange couple did all the talking, and they were not buying his story.

By the time Joe's father got home, Joe admitted that he was using. His father was blown away and tried to deny it, but the evidence was there, including Joe's confession that he was using. Joe was furious at his mother and those strangers; he knew his father would never have found out or believed his mother if it had not been for them. His mother had said that she wanted Joe to go for an assessment, and those strangers had talked his father into it.

So, as Joe stood in the reception room of the treatment center with his parents, he thought the whole thing was stupid and senseless. He admitted that he used drugs, but he was no worse than the people he hung around with. Joe could not admit, even to himself, how scared he was; not just of being there, but of being a failure. He used drugs to cover up those feelings of inadequacy and guilt—inadequate because he could never be as good as he thought his dad wanted him to be, and guilt because he knew that he was all show and no go. Joe also could not admit that even though he made a big deal out of partying, his using was really out of control, and having to cover up using and dealing made him hate himself. Joe could not admit those things now, but he did know that when he was coming down, he felt anxious and awful, and the only way to counteract those feelings was to use. So Joe looked around the reception room with a superior expression, feeling stone cold inside except for the feeling that he really would like to smoke a joint.

TEENAGE CHEMICAL DEPENDENCY

"Everybody uses drugs. All of my friends drink. Kids have to experiment. I don't have a problem with drugs. I can maintain. I know when to quit. Kids will be kids." Those are some of the things young people and parents say to minimize what is going on with drugs and alcohol. Dean, Connie, Joe, and their parents all said similar things, but the young people *were*, in fact, in trouble with drugs. Even though the three may seem to have very different stories, they are really the same. The addictive process goes through four stages from experimentation to dependency.

Experimentation

The period of experimentation is often very short; as soon as a decision is made to stop or to continue using the substance, experimentation is over. Dean's experimentation with alcohol ended when he made the decision to drink his dad's bourbon and ginger when Dad was unaware of it. His experimentation with drugs ended when he reached junior high. Before that, he had not gone looking for pot even though he liked the way it made him feel, but once he began using with his buddies at school his decision was made and experimentation was over.

Connie moved out of experimentation with alcohol when she decided, at a very young age, to make herself a drink when she made her dad one. As far as other drugs were concerned, Connie did not bother to experiment. That first party with Merry and the gang had her off and running.

Since he had lots of practice experimenting at home, it was not difficult for Joe to decide to use alcohol as soon as he became an athlete in junior high. Pot and partying went together, and Joe was a party person. He had no problem making the decision to use pot on a regular basis.

Early Stage

The early stage of chemical use is marked by increase in the young person's tolerance; it takes more beer to get a buzz on or more marijuana to feel high. There is boasting about being able to "maintain" or "handle it." Use increases: getting high at school, cutting class to get high, drinking during the week. Grades go down; perhaps the person is suspended; there is a lack of interest in school activities; parents begin to notice changes in behavior, and arguments start. The teenager begins to be preoccupied with partying or using. On Monday morning the topic of conversation is: "Where's the party going to be next weekend?" because Friday brings "party hardy" time.

This stage is also when the teenager begins drinking and using alone and may experience blackouts. Planning where and with whom to get high and how to be sure to have enough "stuff" becomes a preoccupation, and using acid, speed, barbs, dust, and cocaine increases. At this point there may not be dependency, but there is definitely harmful involvement.

The time it takes to reach harmful involvement varies from person to person; however, it takes much less time for a teenager than for an adult. Some teens, like Connie, get there in just a few weeks; others, like Joe, take a year. But once they reach this point, it is very difficult to turn around because they have progressed to the middle stage of chemical use.

Middle Stage

Getting high is where it's at, and getting high every day or almost every day is the only way to go. Being high becomes normal, and getting the money for drugs of number one importance. Stealing and lying are a way of life, and dealing may become necessary to take care of increased tolerance and the need to stay high. Not everyone has to steal, but even Joe, who had plenty of money from his parents, had to lie and deal to get the money he needed. Without such resources, Dean had to get into some big-time stealing, but a part of that was the exitement and rush he got from the risk he was taking. Poor Connie did not always have to have money, but she lost her self-respect by trading it to boys and men for drugs.

The user begins to get careless during this stage and begins to show up in court as Dean did. Joe totaled his car, and Connie began running away to avoid confrontations at home. Dean and Connie were all but out of school because their using friends were not school-oriented. Joe maintained in school because he was still motivated by sports, and all of his using friends were also the "popular," well-to-do kids who liked to party.

Part of the user's carelessness may show up in being caught with drugs or paraphernalia or in coming home drunk or stoned. Many parents do not know what to look for as far as paraphernalia is concerned, and some are so ignorant that the teen can smoke weed at home and the parent does not recognize the odor. Connie had to have been obviously stoned, but her parents did not recognize it. Joe came home drunk and got a "boys will be boys" type bawling out from his father. Dean was in trouble with the law, but his parents were not looking for drugs. Teens use drugs and alcohol, on the average, for at least two years before parents find the first signs. By that time, like Joe, Dean, and Connie, the teen is deeply involved and may be in the last stage.

Final Stage

The final stage of chemical use is using to feel normal. Feeling high is the only normal way to feel anymore. Physically the drugs take a toll. Connie looked like a scarecrow; Dean was thin, coughed all the time, and was having flashbacks; coke was making Joe's nose run, and he was getting a marijuana cough as well. If they were going to "shoot up," this would be the time, and Dean was giving it more and more thought.

All three teens had lost control over their use. They might say they were not going to get drunk, but they always ended up drunk. Joe was going to cut down on his use, but he could not control the urge. Standing in the reception room of the treatment center, he wanted to use; the urge was overwhelming.

Thoughts of suicide are not unusual in chemically dependent teens, and Dean and Connie had both given it some thought. As much as they hated themselves, Joe hated himself, but he still had some self-esteem that kept him going. All three had lots of pain to face and work through if they were to get well.

While the teenagers were progressing through the stages of chemical use, their parents were progressing through the stages of their co-dependency.

CHAPTER VII

Co-dependency of Parents
of Chemically Dependent Teens

When the Niles, Vivials, and Jocques agreed to put their sons and daughter into treatment, they also agreed to attend family meetings as well. At one of the meetings, Tom and Trudy Tippical told the story of the nightmare their family went through before their son got into treatment.

The Tippicals were a very ordinary family. They had three children and Troy was the middle child. Whenever he seemed to be having difficulty, they figured it was because he was the one in the middle. All through school Troy had done reasonably well until he got into junior high. The D in world history made his first report card a disappointment, but he claimed that his history teacher did not like him and was unfair. When Trudy called the teacher, she found out that Troy had been late for class five times and had missed two important quizzes as a result; therefore, his grade was lowered. Trudy asked the teacher if Troy could make up the quizzes, but Mr. Global refused. Trudy felt that he was being unfair. Maybe Troy had been late, but he should have been allowed to make up the quizzes.

Trudy agreed not to tell his father about the D if Troy promised to work hard and bring the grade up by the next report card. Troy promised faithfully that he would get to class on time and study harder. When the next report card was sent home, there were two Ds besides an F in world history. Trudy could not, nor did she want to, hide this report card from Tom. This was totally unacceptable, and Tom and Trudy both went to the school for conferences with the teachers. All three teachers said that Troy was late for class and was disruptive. Trudy and Tom were eager to cooperate with the teachers and made arrangements to be given a weekly progress report on Troy's behavior as well as his academic work. They checked with Troy every night to be sure that he had completed his homework. The first two weeks Troy brought home the progress report signed by each of his teachers, and things seemed to be going better. The third week Troy said he forgot to pick up the paper in the office and take it around. Mr. Rule, the dean, had made it clear that the responsibility for getting the report signed each week was Troy's, that if he forgot or refused to take it to each teacher, no one would remind him or get a report for him. Tom and Trudy were very unhappy with Troy because he had forgotten the report and grounded him for the weekend. The next week when the progress report was not brought home, Troy said he had left it in his locker at school. This time he was restricted for a full week, not just the weekend.

Schoolwork was not the only kind of work that the Tippicals were trying to get Troy to do. It was a constant struggle to get him to do anything around the house, and his room resembled a toxic waste site. Trudy tried every way she knew to get Troy to take out the garbage and put his dirty dishes in the dishwasher, but all she got was silence or smart backtalk. Troy was really beginning to get a mouth on him, and she hated it when he told her she was a nag. She knew that adolescence was a difficult time and that teen rebellion was common, so she tried to be understanding and not be too upset.

Tom was not so concerned about the chores not being done, but when the family got together for the holidays and Troy had to be forced to go to his uncle's for Christmas dinner, he was very upset. Even more upsetting was Troy's sneaking out on New Year's Eve when both sets of his grandparents were over for the evening. He came back about an hour before everyone left and hurried to bed so that Tom could not make a scene in front of the family. By the time his grandparents had left, Troy was fast asleep, and Trudy asked Tom not to wake him.

Tom had been really angry because he was embarrassed when he went to find Troy and realized that the boy had slipped out. He had covered it up by saying that he forgot Troy had been invited to a friend's house for the evening, but, all the same, Tom had been embarrassed. It was not to be the last time that he was embarrassed by the behavior of his son.

Getting Troy through seventh grade with passing grades had

made that spring a trying time for Trudy and Tom. Conferences and phone calls were a standard part of Trudy's life. With each passing week Troy seemed to become more rebellious and irritable. The slightest thing sent him into a black mood. It was so frustrating and confusing. They were doing their best to be good parents, and Troy seemed to become more and more difficult to handle.

If the Tippicals thought spring was bad, summer was worse. Troy slept until at least noon, got up, showered, ate something and took off, not to be seen again until midnight or later. Trudy had been frantic the first few times Troy had not shown up for dinner and had not called. By ten o'clock the first night, Tom had been worried enough to call the emergency room at the hospital. Finally, at half past twelve, Troy had come home, and the first of a regular series of nasty arguments had taken place. Troy accused his parents of not trusting him and of treating him like a baby. Put on the defensive, Trudy and Tom found themselves justifying their right as parents to expect consideration and cooperation with reasonable rules from a young teenager. They ended up frustrated and unhappy while Troy felt justified in his inconsiderate, irresponsible behavior.

As the summer wore on, there were nights when Troy did not come home at all. At first Tom and Trudy were frantic and called everyone they could think of to see if Troy were with friends. People were irritated by being awakened after midnight, and the Tippicals were shocked to find out that most of the people Troy had said he was seeing had not had contact with him for months. That revelation made the Tippicals wonder whom he actually *was* with, and it created a new dimension to their argument when Troy finally did get home.

Troy refused to bring any of his friends home, and he also refused to tell his parents who they were. Trudy had been so determined to find out who these people were that she listened in on phone calls and followed Troy to see where he went. He caught her following him and went into an uncontrolled rage. She was afraid he might hit her, and he threatened to do just that if she followed him again. It was a week before he came home.

Summer finally ended, and Trudy thought things would settle down when Troy got back into school. Teachers began calling her the second week of school. When a teacher was not calling, the dean was—to tell her that Troy had been kicked out of class again. When Troy got four Ds and three Fs on his first report card, Trudy and Tom talked it over and decided that the teachers must have gotten together to give him a hard time. Troy claimed that none of them liked him and would never give him any help. Trudy had talked to them on the telephone so many times that she was sure that all of their complaints could not be true. The Tippicals agreed that Tom should take Troy to school the next day and talk to Mr. Rule about changing Troy's class schedule.

Within two weeks Trudy was getting phone calls again. This time Troy was cutting classes. He did not come back to school after lunch; he did not get to school until third period; he was not at school at all on Friday. Not wanting to admit that she did not know where her son was, Trudy said that Troy had a doctor's appointment after lunch and had forgotten the note that day and also the day he went to the dentist and did not get to school until third period. Feeling guilty but not knowing what else to do, Trudy covered for his absences by saying Troy was sick. She did not tell Tom what she was doing, and when she said anything to Troy about cutting school, he told her it was none of her business.

Getting Troy out of bed in the morning was a real chore, and Trudy battled with him every morning. She was determined that he was going to get to school every day and on time, so she started driving him to school and leaving him off right at the door. What Trudy did not know was that after Troy walked in the front door, he walked out the back door to meet his buddies.

Conditions at home were getting worse and worse. Troy absolutely refused to do anything around the house or to participate in family activities in any way. Tom and Trudy had finally given up insisting that he go places with the family. They had tried reasoning with him and punishing him and only ended up arguing with him. Their arguments were getting louder and more heated all the time. Finally, in desperation, they went to a child psychiatrist who had been highly recommended.

When she took him for the first session with the psychiatrist, Troy said he would not talk, making Trudy feel more anxious and concerned than ever. After the session was over, Troy's whole attitude about the psychiatrist was different, and he said he thought Dr. Addle was "real cool." Trudy breathed a sigh of relief and felt sure that things would begin to get better. After two months of weekly sessions, Dr. Addle called Trudy and Tom in and told them that Troy's major problem centered around them and how they were handling him during this trying time of transition into adulthood. When all was said and done, he asserted, Troy did not have a problem, they did; and until they took care of their problems, there would be little improvement for Troy.

Trying to be the best parents possible, Tom and Trudy went to therapy for a year, but things did not improve with Troy. In fact, they kept getting worse. No one suspected drugs as the underlying cause of Troy's behavior. One time he did come home drunk, but that was excused as teenage experimentation. A few other times Trudy suspected that he might have been drinking, but since she could not be sure, she did not want to accuse him. Neither Trudy nor Tom had any knowledge of how other drugs affect behavior, so they did not know what to look for and did not recognize the signs when they were present.

Trudy noticed that Troy was having more colds and seemed to have a bad cough that hung on. His eyes were watery, but that was nothing new since he had allergies; however, the allergies did seem to be getting worse.

The major problem the Tippicals struggled with was Troy's trouble with the law. He had been picked up for shoplifting, but they had managed to take care of that by talking the store manager out of pressing charges and paying for the merchandise that Troy had taken. When he was arrested for vandalism, they paid the restitution cost; but when he was arrested for bicycle theft, the judge put Troy in juvenile hall for six weeks.

Visiting days were a horror for Trudy and Tom. They hated to see Troy in there with all those rough, mean boys. He did not belong there. They were sure that those boys would be a bad influence or would even hurt him. In addition to their fear and anxiety, Troy spent the entire visiting times telling them how his being there was their fault. He said they had gotten him a lousy lawyer because they were too cheap to pay for a good one, that they never gave him things so he had to steal to get what he wanted, that they were bad parents just as Dr. Addle had said all along.

Each time Tom left with jaws clenched in anger, and Trudy cried all the way home. She felt guilty and personally responsible for Troy's being in that horrible place. If only she had known what to do. She *should* have known what to do. She was heartbroken and it was her own fault! For Tom it was humiliating having to visit his son in that place, and he felt guilty because he had not been able to keep Troy from "going wrong." But mostly, he felt angry. Troy had no right to say the things he did. Parents should not have to put up with that from a child. After all they had done for him, Troy appreciated nothing and could only criticize and complain. The question in Tom's mind was, "What kind of monster have I created?" Tom and Trudy loved their son, but that did not seem to be enough.

When Troy got out of the hall and Trudy took him to school, she was informed that he had been transferred to the continuation high school. Trudy was upset about that and knew that Tom would be too, but she did not see what she could do about it; so she enrolled Troy in the continuation school. That evening when Tom got home and was upset about the change in schools, Troy informed them that it did not make any difference because he was not going to school anyway. Tom was like an erupting volcano, and Troy called him some obscene names and stomped out the door.

After two weeks of constant fighting over school and Troy's refusal to go, the Tippicals finally gave up trying to make him go, but they did not give up worrying about what would happen to him in the future without an education. Not being able to handle calls from school, Trudy stopped answering the phone during the day unless Tom called and used their agreed-upon code of hanging up after one ring and calling again.

Besides worrying about Troy's not going to school and wondering what he did all day, Trudy was worried about his health. He was so thin and did not eat much at all. She tried to cook things that she knew he liked, but he would eat a few bites and that was it. Trudy wanted to take him in for a checkup and made appointments for him, but he never came home in time to go to the doctor. She was frantic with worry.

Troy began to come and go as he pleased, using the house as a hotel. The phone rang at all hours of the night, and some nights Tom and Trudy could hear Troy leaving. He had no regard whatsoever for the rest of the family and stole anything that was not locked up. He even took his younger sister's stereo that her grandparents had given her for having perfect attendance in sixth grade. When he was confronted about it, Troy picked up a chair and smashed it into the glass-enclosed case that held Trudy's collection of ceramic owls, breaking half of the figurines that she had been collecting since she was a little girl.

Then one day when Trudy was going through pockets before washing Troy's clothes, she found a half-filled plastic bag of what looked like green weeds and another bag with white powder in it. Even though she had never seen it before, Trudy was sure the "weeds" were marijuana and that the white powder was some other drug. With shaking hands, she took the bags to the kitchen, picked up the phone, and called Tom. He was home in less than a half hour and found her sitting in the living room, tears streaming down her face. What she had feared for so long was true. She could no longer ignore the nagging suspicions she had felt for over a year when she saw grass and weed traces in the pockets of Troy's pants and shirts and the funny "vases" under his bed and in his closet. She had wondered if he were beginning some kind of collection of little pipes, disregarding the little voice in her head that reminded her of the pictures in the paper a year ago of pipes that were being sold in "head shops." Trudy was devastated, and there was no consoling her.

They sat up until three in the morning waiting for Troy to come home, and when they showed him what Trudy had found, he started screaming obscenities and lunged for the drugs. Trudy, off balance, was knocked down. Tom went into a fury and told Troy to get out and never come back. Troy sneered back that they could not kick him out of his own house because he was under eighteen, but he was not staying in this *&##%&* house any longer.

Feeling hopeless, helpless, and completely defeated, Tom and Trudy did not know what to do next. Trudy was sure she was a bad person and that God was punishing her for some horrible thing she had done. Though she had always gone to church, she now became extremely devout, read her Bible every day, joined a prayer group, and became solemn, serious, and almost rigid. Tom did not understand what had happened to her, and he felt abandoned and isolated. At times he hated Troy because Trudy was so preoccupied with him, and he blamed Troy for making him feel like such a failure as a parent.

The next time Tom and Trudy saw Troy was in juvenile court. He had been arrested for breaking and entering. When the call came, Trudy told the officer that Troy had not been at home for nine weeks; she asked him to call Tom at work because Tom had told her he would not allow Troy back in the house. As Trudy expected, Tom told the officer that he would not go down and get Troy. He did not even want to hire a lawyer to defend Troy, but Trudy got so upset that he did call a lawyer.

The Tippicals, asked why Troy was no longer living at home, told of finding the drugs and of Troy's behavior when he had been confronted. Their interview was put into the court report, and when Troy went before the judge he was ordered to enter a drug treatment program.

When their story was finished, the Tippicals told the parent group that entering the treatment facility was the beginning, not the end. Looking back on what had gone on while Troy was progressing through his addiction, they could see how very sick they had become; and their illness had progressed through the same stages as Troy's. They had learned about their illness and Troy's and now had new ways of looking at themselves and at him.

STAGES IN CO-DEPENDENCE OF PARENTS

Early Stage

When young people begin using drugs, their parents become "reactive." Because the behavior of the teen changes, the parents react to the behavior. During the experimental stage of drug use, not enough of the chemical is used to bring about changes in behavior, so there are no changes in the parents' behavior either. As the teen gets into a regular using pattern, behavior begins to change, usually showing up first in school with minor behavior problems and a dip in academic performance. The parents react to this by contacting teachers to see what is happening. Often, as Trudy did, mothers cover for the young person because they do not want Father to overreact and punish the teen more severely than they feel is warranted. Sooner or later, though, the grades or the behavior deteriorates to the point where Father must be told.

Parents try to be as helpful and cooperative as possible, so they set up daily or weekly checks with teachers and vow to see that the homework is done. They set rules for TV viewing or telephone privileges based on how much time they think the teen needs to work on homework every night. They become more and more concerned about school as the teen becomes less and less interested.

Combined with the worries about school is the lack of cooperation at home. Chores are skipped or done sloppily, and mothers become nags. Sometimes it is the perfectionistic fathers who demand much more than their offspring cares to give. When the teen begins to balk at going to family gatherings and doing things with the family, tension builds. Parents force the teen to go to Grandma's or to go out for ice cream with the rest of the family.

With the tug of war created by *You are going with us—I don't want to go* comes the drawing up of battle lines. When that is added to the conflict over school, the power struggle is on.

At this stage parents are confused and frustrated and are beginning to be embarrassed by some of the teen's behavior. Fathers are frequently angry because they are not being obeyed, and mothers are concerned because things are not going smoothly.

Middle Stage

As the teen gets more and more involved with the use of drugs, with other drug users, and with the business of obtaining drugs, less and less attention is paid to school, home, and people in general. For the user, life revolves around drugs. For parents, life revolves around the user. They begin to go to any lengths to get the young person to go to school. Trudy covered Troy's truancies to keep him out of trouble at school, woke him up every day and took him to the school door to be sure he got there. Tom demanded that his schedule be changed to teachers who were not against him.

When Troy began staying out late, the Tippicals stayed up and confronted him, causing a big fight. When he did not come home at all, they frantically called people. Trudy was typical of parents in this stage when she followed Troy. Parents often drive around and around searching for the teen. When the user finds out about it, there is a horrible argument. Trying to reason with the user is like talking to the plant being smoked and leads to more arguing. The verbal abuse from both sides is destructive and devastating.

Some parents believe the old saw, "If you can't beat them, join them" and they try to be a buddy. That is fine as long as the teen user is getting what he wants, but if a parent's "buddiness" gets in the way—watch out! Some parents who are aware that the teen is smoking pot say, "I don't want you sneaking out to smoke pot. You can do it at home," and they sit down and smoke with the teen. That is real cool, but the parents soon find that their private reserve of marijuana disappears very quickly, and the behavior of the teenager does not improve. Being a buddy does not help the situation any more than being a dictator.

When the teen abuser gets in trouble with the law, parents are usually protective and do not want the youngster in jail. Even the third time they are called by juvenile authorities to come and get a teen who has been picked up, they feel that their child is different from the usual inmate in juvenile center. They believe he really did not do it. They will hire an attorney, pay the fine, make restitution, beg people not to press charges, promise to "make it up" to people—in short, they will do anything to "help" their son or daughter.

Often the school or the juvenile justice system strongly urges the parents to seek family counseling. If the counselor is not enlightened about chemical dependency, it is easy for the teen user to play games with him. Some counselors believe that drug use is a symptom of an underlying emotional problem, and that when you solve the underlying problem the drug use will stop. Drug users love that philosophy and, like Troy with Dr. Addle, weave a tale of parent misunderstanding and mistreatment that gets them off the hook immediately. Also, it is not unusual for a teen user to lie when asked by a psychologist if he uses. Then the psychologist moves on to the "real" emotional issue that needs to be worked through. Emotional problems cannot be handled by a brain clouded by drugs that cripple the very part of it that must be used to deal with emotional issues. *The drug use must be stopped first.*

As a result of taking Troy to a psychiatrist who was unenlightened, Trudy and Tom went through a year of therapy that allowed Troy's disease to progress unchecked while they tried to work through problems they were unable to deal with because they were suffering from active co-dependency. Their sick reactive behavior continued in spite of therapy.

The pain and humiliation of feeling responsible for the behavior of the chemical abuser is no greater than the pain and humiliation of the parents' own behavior. Loving, kind, considerate people who have turned into screaming monsters do not feel good about themselves. They doubt their worth as parents and as human beings.

Late Stage

By the time the teen reaches the final stage of addiction, the parents are at their wits' end. They have tried everything they can think of, and things keep getting worse. They give up trying to get the teen to go to school, but many still try to control things like hair, clothes, and comings and goings and still argue about behavior, lying, stealing, drug and alcohol use, and sleazy friends. Parents search for the drug supply and throw out what they find. They mark their own liquor bottles or try to hide them. Sometimes parents ignore teen users and refuse to talk to or be in the same room with them.

The verbal abuse on both sides is incredible, and often parents resort to physical abuse because they are so desperate to stop what is happening. When the teen leaves because of the tension and constant fighting, parents are relieved because the source of the tension is gone, but the anxiety of not knowing if the teen is safe tears them up.

In spite of all the rage and bad feelings, when a teen gets into serious trouble with the law, parents still try to get him off. It is as though they are driven to push the user out of their lives on the one hand, and to protect and hold on as tightly as possible on the other.

Hopeless, helpless, and in despair, parents feel like failures as parents and as people. They find it difficult to be with others, especially friends who they feel are good parents and whose children are doing well. Mothers may get sick and go to bed. Some co-dependents cannot get up in the morning, they are so depressed. Some turn to religion to help them survive the wreckage they see their lives to be.

A horrifying feeling of hatred for their own child overwhelms some parents, causing them to feel guilty. They do not stop to think that they would probably hate anyone who treated them as the chemically dependent one is treating them; they just feel like bad people for feeling the way they do. They have additional guilt as a result of their feelings of responsibility for the behavior of the youth. They feel that parents "should" be able to control their children, and that self-imposed "should" heaps piles of guilt on them and is added to by a society that tells them they did a bad job or their child would be okay.

Additional guilt is suffered because parents know they are neglecting the other children in the family, yet they do not have time to attend to the others who are usually managing to get along all right. In some families, the user influences younger children to become involved with drugs, even introducing them to their first high. With two or more users in the family, the parents' co-dependency is more marked, and they may very well give up and stop trying to be parents.

Older Chemically Dependent Youth

Not all teenage chemical abusers start using at such a young age, and even if they do, they may not get treatment for their addiction. There are many confused, resentful parents who do not know that the nineteen-year-old or twenty-three-year-old sitting on the couch watching TV every day is chemically dependent. They just know that they have an able-bodied offspring who is not working, not doing any work in the house, not contributing to the family in any way, but who demands to come and go as he pleases and wants first-class service. The young person may or may not have finished high school, but the jobs open to him are limited. He refuses to work in a fast-food place, or else he is working in one and complaining about not having enough money, expecting Mom and Dad to come up with more.

Caught up in their co-dependency, parents see no way to get the young person to be self-sufficient. The youth is not going to make an effort to do anything because things are comfortable at home. He may have to put up with nagging and complaining, but he can get away with his buddies for a while in the evening and still know that he has a place to eat and sleep and get a few bucks when he needs it. He knows his parents will never turn him out, and he has it made.

Without help, the family will be trapped in dependency and co-dependency indefinitely.

GETTING HELP FOR THE FAMILY

A variety of agencies for families exist in any community. Any family member can start the family on its way to recovery by finding help. School counselors and nurses can put you in touch with people in the community who can help. Alcohol and drug treatment centers have employees who will answer your questions and talk with you or your parents. Look in the yellow pages under Alcoholism or Drug Abuse for listings of programs in your community. Almost all of them will be willing to answer questions and talk with you. The National Council on Alcoholism frequently has volunteer counselors to listen and help you. Besides regular Al-Anon groups, some cities have groups for parents of teen chemical abusers. Alateen groups are for teens who have family members or friends who are alcoholic, and most teen drug abusers are also alcoholic. A Toughlove Parent Support Group in your area can help your parents and tell you if there is a Toughlove for Kids group that you can attend. There are wonderful, supportive people in your community who will help you and your family.

CHAPTER VIII

Coping with a Drug-abusing Brother or Sister

On the way to her first family day at the treatment center, Joy Jocque felt anxious about what might be expected of her. She was two years older than Joe and had been the first one in the family to know about his using drugs. He had told her about drinking beer in junior high, and she had just brushed it off as "kid stuff" that all the boys tried. When Joe was in eighth grade, he told her about smoking pot, and at first she would ask him what it was like, because she had never tried it. It was sort of exciting to hear his stories about how he felt and the way everything looked, but after a while Joy began to realize that Joe was really getting involved with marijuana.

Joy had always felt close to Joe and considered her little brother to be someone special. Loving her brother, being good to him, and feeling responsible for him were an important part of who Joy was. She had always been a superresponsible person and liked the feeling of control she had over her world as well as the approval she got from adults.

Pleasing her parents and doing things that made them happy were number one in her life; consequently, Joy got straight As in school and did everything she could to be as perfect as possible. If her mother asked her to do something, she did it, and any words of disapproval from either of her parents put her in tears.

As Joe got more and more into drugs and began arguing with their mother, Joy could not understand it. She would never have considered raising her voice to her mother, and when they fought Joy would cry. Joe would tell her that it was none of her business, the arguments had nothing to do with her, so there was no reason for her to cry. Her mother would tell her that she needed to learn to control her emotions, that there was no reason for her to be crying. Joy got so that she would hold back her tears until she could get to her friend Kay's house. Without Kay,

Joy did not know what she would have done. Kay would listen and pat her on the back while she cried, not offering any advice because there was none to give, just listening.

Many times Kay invited Joy to stay for dinner, but Joy always said that she had to be home for dinner. With things so bad at home and Joy knowing there would be arguing at the dinner table, Kay could not understand why Joy felt that she had to be there. Joy could not explain it, but a part of her told her that somehow she could control the situation by being there, that things would be worse if she were not there. Since Joy was the hero in the family, she felt it was her job to make things better, and being there would make things better during dinner. So any night her brother was at home Joy had a totally miserable dinner.

As Joe went on using, he began doing destructive, uncaring things at home. It seemed to Joy that the worse Joe became, the more her father catered to him. Giving Joe the TransAm for his sixteenth birthday was almost more than Joy could stand. When she had graduated first in her class the June before, her father had given her the three-year-old Ford and bought her mother a new car. Joe merely had to exist until he was sixteen to get a TransAm. She really resented the way her father played down Joe's bad behavior. Since he worked sixty or more hours a week, he was never home to see how Joe treated their mother. He was never home to be a part of the family at all, and when he was at home he sat in front of the TV with a drink in his hand. She had seen him come home bombed more than once, and she was concerned about his drinking and resentful that he did not see what was happening with Joe. All her father cared about was football; as long as Joe's grades were high enough to keep him eligible and he was a star on the football team, her father did not care what else Joe did. But let her get one B and he wanted to know why she was letting her grades slip.

When Joe totaled the TransAm, Joy was hoping her parents would take it as a warning that something was wrong. She could not believe it when they got him the Corvette. He became even more unbearable after that, and seemed to care less and less how his behavior affected her or their mother. He came and went as he pleased, and he began taking money from her. Until then she had not noticed money missing, but after he got the Corvette, Joy found that money disappeared from her wallet and from the jar she kept things in. She knew that Joe knew where she kept her money, so asked him if he had taken it. He denied it, but later when she told him instead of asking him, he admitted the truth.

Joy had covered for Joe for years. When he was supposed to mow the lawn and did not, she would do it so her parents would not get angry. When Joe was late, he would tap on her window and she would let him in the back door so her parents would not know how late he was. If he cut a class and the teacher asked her if he was sick, she would always cover for him. Sometimes when he had a paper due and put it off until the last minute, Joy would stay up late and type it for him so it would be in on time. Joe was her brother and she loved him. She knew that he took advantage of her, but she could not stop helping him.

At times, Joe's lack of consideration made Joy angry. She had some big sweaters that she liked real well, and Joe took them without asking. When she complained and told him not to wear her sweaters, he said she was making a big deal out of nothing. One time he took her favorite sweatshirt and cut the sleeves out. His only comment was, "What's the big?" He did not seem to care about anything but himself.

Because she did not want her mother to get angry and fight with Joe, Joy did her best to talk him out of doing things she knew her mother would not like. He told her to mind her own business and called her names. "Goody-goody" was one of his favorites, along with "Kissy-kissy" and some others that she did not like to think about. He made fun of her "straight-arrow friends who thought they were too good to party." He accused her of always trying to make him look bad, told her he knew she did not trust him and that it was a pretty sick way to treat her own brother. If he could not insult her, the guilt trip usually worked. Any time Joy tried to stand up to Joe, he yelled and swore and she ended up crying. Then he would stomp off disgusted, telling her she was a loser and impossible to reason with.

The more Joy covered for her brother and tried to smooth things over with her parents, the more she resented Joe. He did not appreciate a thing she did for him, yet he kept taking advantage of her. Even though she knew he lied and cheated and stole, she could not stop thinking that if she tried hard enough, he would appreciate what she did and treat her better. She wanted his approval as badly as she wanted that of her parents and other people, but the more she did, the less Joe seemed to care about her.

As her mother seemed to focus more and more on Joe and her father thought only of his future pro football star, Joy felt more and more left out of the family. She tried so hard to do well and to be noticed, but all she got was a "That's good" when she brought her report card home. She was awarded a full scholarship to a nearby women's college when she graduated from high school, and her father carried on for weeks because she was not going to the private university he had chosen for her. He said he was embarrassed by the scholarship, that people would think he could not pay for his own kid's education. He was especially angry because she had not told anyone in the family that she had applied for the scholarship.

When Joy had applied for the scholarship, she had known that her parents would disapprove of the school, and she did not want to go through the hassle of telling them. She had given up trying to talk to them two years ago. When she had wanted to talk, they were not interested, or they got angry and she heard about it for weeks afterward. Her policy was not to talk about anything important to her at home and not to talk about home to outsiders except Kay. The people in her home were not safe to talk to about herself, and she did not want anyone outside to know what her family was like.

Once Joy had tried to talk to her mother about Joe, but the best she could do was to say that he was running with a pretty rowdy crowd. Her mother had assured her that all of Joe's friends came from nice families and would not get into any trouble. There was no way Joy could make herself tell her mother what she knew about Joe. She could not break the No-Talk Rule about his using any more than she could talk about how worried she was about her father's drinking. Even though he was seldom home, when her father was there he drank a lot. Joy had been there when he came in late some nights, and she could tell that he had been drinking. She never mentioned it to her mother, and her mother never mentioned it to her. Knowing her father's reaction ahead of time, Joy never mentioned her concerns to him.

Keeping all of her concerns to herself had become the rule for Joy because she did not trust anyone in her family to respect them and treat them with consideration. No one talked and no one trusted—themselves or each other. The Don't-Trust Rule was in effect in the Jocque household, and the Don't-Feel Rule was becoming more and more necessary as the pain in the family grew.

Joy covered her feelings of disappointment, inadequacy, fear, and anger with tears. Everything was expressed as sadness. When she was at home, there was so much pain in her life that it was easier just to shut down; and that shut out the good feelings of happiness, enthusiasm, cheerfulness, and pleasure. Soon Joy had lost the good feelings outside of the house too. She still worked really hard for other people's approval, but no matter how hard she worked and how much approval she got, it was never enough. She was never able to do enough to make things better at home, to make her feel better about herself.

When Joy found out that her mother was going to Toughlove parent group meetings, she was relieved that someone was finally trying to do something about Joe. The day her mother asked her if Joe was using drugs, Joy had not known what to do. She knew she had to tell the truth, and she had wanted her parents to know for a long time; but she still felt that she had betrayed Joe. Then when she found out how her mother had brought another couple in to help search the house and confront Joe, Joy had felt like jumping up and down and shouting. She was so glad that her mother had taken action, but when she saw how angry and hurt Joe looked, she felt guilty and responsible for that. Even though she knew that her mother had known about Joe before asking her, Joy still felt responsible. It did not make sense, but most of what had been happening the past three years did not make sense either.

As she looked out the car window on the way to the drug treatment center, Joy wondered if she would be able to tell the secrets that she had been keeping all this time. Would she just cry, as usual, or would she be able to say how angry she was because of the things Joe had done to her? Would she have an opportunity to tell her parents how left out and overlooked she felt even though she had done her very best to be a perfect daughter and earn their love? Would she be able to tell her father that she wished he were home more and that she was afraid he was drinking too much? Would she be able to say how relieved she feels since she is away at school most of the time and does not have to be in the tension at home? Could she withstand her family's disapproval if they did not like what she said? Could she talk knowing they would disapprove of most of what she said? Staring out the window, seeing nothing, Joy wondered and worried as they sped on toward the treatment center.

Coming from the opposite direction toward the treatment center was Connie Vivial's little brother, Barry, who was nine years old. Barry was not too sure where they were going and what would happen when they got there. He knew Connie was there because of using drugs, but he did not know why he had to go and talk to the people there. He did know that he was glad Connie was not at home, had been glad any time she had run away and was gone. Not having her at home was a big relief.

Even though he was only seven when Connie had started partying with Merry Maiker, Barry knew that Connie had been drinking at home for a long time before that. She drank when they were home alone after school and told him if he told on her she would beat him up. She had pounded on him enough so that Barry knew she could hurt him. He had tried to hit her back a few times, but she was so much bigger that he could not hurt her. Once after he had hit her, Connie had gotten mad and punched him in the stomach and hurt him, so Barry decided not to hit her again until he was big enough to defend himself.

When Connie began partying, she bragged to Barry about how great it was to get high. One time she had some marijuana at home and made him smoke it. He was really scared and held the smoke in his mouth and blew it out as soon as he could. Connie was so busy getting high that she did not notice that he was not doing it right.

Because he was so much younger, Connie did not try to hide anything from Barry. He knew when she was out partying and

came home late. When their parents locked the door thinking
Connie would have to wake them to get in, she had knocked on
his window and Barry had sneaked out and opened the back
door for her. When she ran away, Barry knew where she was
because other kids would tell him they had seen her. If he had
told his parents, Connie would have been mad and beaten him
up, so he kept it to himself. Barry felt bad about keeping secrets
from his parents, but he did not know what else to do.

Knowing how upset his parents were over Connie's behavior,
Barry tried hard to be good. He wanted his parents to notice
how good he was, but all they did was worry about Connie and
yell at her when she was home. Nobody seemed to notice him.
The only time he got any attention was when he did something
bad, but even then he was nowhere near as bad as Connie, so
they did not seem to notice very much. Besides, Barry felt so
guilty when he got into trouble that he went back to being good.

As Connie's attitude got worse as she got more and more into
using drugs, Barry told her that she should not do what she was
doing. He tried to make her see how she was messing things up,
but she told him to mind his own business. She called him a little
creep and yelled at him. Barry yelled back, but he was always
very careful about how mad he made her. He knew just how
much he could say before she hit him. Connie was always in a
bad mood, and it put him in a bad mood too. That is why he
liked to yell back at her so much.

What Barry wanted more than anything was for his parents to
do something about Connie's behavior. She got by with everything and they jumped all over him for nothing. It was not fair!
She stayed out all night and they did nothing about it, but he
was not allowed to watch TV if he came home late from school.
It was really confusing, and he could not understand why they
did not do something to stop Connie. Parents are supposed to
make their children behave. They made him behave, why not
Connie?

Although he loved his parents very much, Barry was angry
with them. He was feeling alone and betrayed and unprotected.
They had really let him down. Since Connie had been in this
treatment place, they had not paid attention to him at all. All
they talked about was what Connie had said on the phone or

what some counselor had said about Connie. Now Barry had to miss school and his roller skating lesson to come down here for Connie. He did not care if he saw her or not. He was glad she was not at home to push him around and tell him what to do.

A short distance behind the Vivials, the Nile family was on the way to the treatment center for family day also. Greg Nile was the same age as Barry Vivial, but his feelings toward Dean were very different from Barry's for Connie. He had kept the same secrets for Dean, but not because he was afraid Dean would hurt him. He loved Dean very much because Dean played catch with him and took him fishing and did all the things big brothers are supposed to do for little brothers. Greg knew that Dean was stealing and dealing, yet he could not tell on his brother because he did not want him to get into trouble. It made no difference that Dean got caught and everyone knew about the burglaries; Greg could not tell what he knew.

Whenever Dean and his mother fought, Greg was very upset because he loved them both. He did not want Dean to treat his mother badly, and he did not want his mother to be angry with Dean. Greg felt as though he were being torn apart. Sometimes he felt that he would have to choose between his mother and his brother, and he could not do that. Most of the time Dean was gone when his father was home, but when they were home together and shouted at each other Greg was really scared because he saw their fists clenched as they stood yelling at each other. He felt so helpless when the fighting was going on. Sometimes he ran into his room and hid. That is exactly what he felt like doing today instead of going to this strange treatment center where Dean was.

Kerrie Nile, who was just a year and a half younger than Dean, had no kind thoughts for him this day. She resented the way he had been interrupting her life for the past three years. Besides that, she was embarrassed to have him for a brother. Kerrie had to go to the same school where Dean was known as a druggie and a loser. No matter how hard she tried or how well she did in school, she could never make up for Dean's disgrace. Beginning in junior high, she had to live down being his sister. For her entire first year of high school she had to watch the surprised look on teacher's faces when they found out that he was her brother. Then following the surprise came the look that told her she would have to try just a little harder to prove that she was not like him. It was no fun being only a year behind him in school.

With all of the mess having to do with Dean's being in trouble, Kerrie did not get the recognition she deserved for doing so well in school. She knew that her parents referred to her as "our A student," but they seemed to take that for granted. They did not seem to realize how hard she worked to prove herself. They gave her one minute for every hour they spend dealing with Dean. He was the mess-up and he got all the attention! It was not fair.

As far as Dean was concerned, Kerrie did not exist, and that was okay with her. She knew what he was doing, had known that he was using drugs from the time he came home from school in seventh grade and told her about getting high. She had not told her parents because she knew how terrible they would feel if they found out that Dean was using drugs. Kerrie had kept her mouth shut about who his friends were and where he was hanging out. When he ran away, she did not tell that Greg knew where he was, even though she knew that Greg had taken clothes to him more than once. Part of the reason she did not tell on him was because Greg had begged her not to. Greg knew everything that was going on; in fact, he had told her where Dean was more than once. Kerrie had always felt protective of Greg, and she could not do anything to make him unhappy; so she helped Dean for Greg's sake. Even so, it did not do any good to help Dean, because he kept getting in trouble anyway. Sometimes Kerrie thought he was just plain stupid. Why else would he do the things he did to himself? Couldn't he see what a mess he was making of his life? Even more than that, she resented the mess he was making of all their lives!

Her parents had tried so hard to do the right things for all of them. Dean did not seem to care how they felt at all. She knew that her parents were not perfect, but they wanted to do what was best for all three of them. Much of her resentment toward Dean was because of his treatment of their parents. Kerrie did not think Dean deserved love and attention from their parents; he had pulled some pretty cruddy stuff on them. He stole money from them and their mother's jewelry; and the way he talked to his mother made Kerrie sick. He never did what they told him to do, and he was such a scummy bum that she did not see how they could stand to be around him.

Dean and Kerrie had had their fights, and she did her best to stay as far away from him as possible now. She had learned her lesson when he borrowed money and promised to pay it back but never did. She got burned more than once before she stopped lending him money. She did not buy any of his lies anymore. After she had come home and found him going through her room, she had never kept anything of value where he could get it. She should have told her parents to do the same thing then, and they would not have lost so much to Dean's stealing. She had tried to talk to him and tell him how he was hurting their parents, but he told her to butt out of his life; so she did just that. Kerrie stayed as far away from Dean as she possibly could. He had not been home much for a long time, and when he was, he ignored her and that was fine with her.

Another great resentment Kerrie had was the way Dean treated Greg. Sure, he played catch with him and took him fishing once in a while, but he took advantage of him because he knew that Greg worshiped the ground he walked on and would do anything for him. He exposed Greg to all of his sleazy friends, and they probably used drugs and made deals right in front of him. Kerrie was sure that Greg knew where the gang took the stuff they stole and who the person was who paid them for it. She knew Greg was not mixed up in the burglaries, but he knew all about them, and she was furious that Dean would expose a little kid like Greg to that kind of low-life stuff.

As the family rode silently toward the treatment center, Kerrie wondered what to expect. Her parents were obviously nervous, and watching Greg stare out the window Kerrie was sure he was not seeing a thing. She wanted to have an open mind, but the big ball of fear and resentment in her stomach told her that this was going to be a hard day.

Early Stage Co-dependency of Siblings

Just as the parents' co-dependency progresses along with the dependency of the young person, the same thing happens with siblings (brothers and sisters.) In the beginning, siblings of drug users know what is going on but say nothing about it. They often get a second-hand thrill out of the stories they hear, much as Joy Jocque did. It is not until the problems with grades or with behavior at home or school arise that brothers and sisters begin to get worried.

Since most brothers and sisters argue and fuss with each other, the arguing that goes on in the early stages of drug use is not much worse than usual. The difference seems to be the reasons for arguing. The user is very touchy and grouchy for no reason, and the sibling does not seem able to avoid the arguments. Younger children are picked on quite a lot.

The early stage is mainly a time of covering for the drug user. This is known as "enabling" because it lets the person continue using without suffering any bad consequences as a result. Siblings do not want the user to get into trouble, or they do not want their parents to get upset. By making it easier for the user to continue using, they are actually causing more pain for both sibling and parents. It is very difficult to tell parents that a brother or sister is using drugs. Nobody wants to be a narc, but families can be saved a lot of heartache if parents are informed early on. If siblings cannot tell their parents about a brother's drug use, they can tell a counselor at school and ask that the information be passed on to their parents. They can talk to a minister or to another adult they trust. If they feel they cannot tell their parents themselves, they can have someone else help them tell their parents. Covering for brothers or sisters does not help them or anyone else. It enables the disease of chemical dependency to get a hold on everyone.

Middle Stage Co-dependency of Siblings

Things begin to heat up as the user gets into his drinking and using. The sibling sees how the user is messing up and starts telling him he ought to shape up. If the user is younger, this usually results in shouting matches or actual physical fighting. If they are evenly matched, the wrestling and fighting become common occurrences that upset parents terribly.

When younger siblings start telling older ones that they are messing up or that they should or should not do something, they usually end up being threatened or hit. Younger ones get into the pattern of irritating the user as Barry did Connie. They try to gauge it so that they do not make the user mad enough to pound on them. Sometimes they miscalculate and get a good thrashing.

The enabling behavior continues during the middle stage of co-dependency because things are such a mess and the sibling has covered for so long that if he tells, the user may hurt him. Also, like Kerrie, the sibling does not want to see their parents hurt any more than they are already. Sometimes, as in Joy's case, they just cannot talk to their parents. They cannot betray their brother even though they see what the drug use is doing. The sibling knows that the failing grades in school and all the other trouble is because of drug use; that all the broken rules and cruddy behavior at home are because of using drugs; that all the sleazy behavior is drug-related, yet the sibling cannot narc on the user.

Some siblings have a feeling of loyalty to their using brother or sister because they are having difficulty getting along with their parents, too. In that case, they side with the user even when they know that he is doing bad things outside of the house. They will be strong allies and cover for the user, lie for him, and keep him out of trouble at home if they can. Sometimes, like Greg Nile, they just love the user so much that they cannot do anything they think will hurt him. They may be angry about what is happening, but they push the angry feelings away as much as they can.

The horrible thing for co-dependent siblings is the terrible feeling of helplessness and disloyalty. They cannot narc, yet they feel that their parents should know. The secret is so heavy that they feel weighed down. Youngsters under ten do not realize what a load they are carrying. "Why don't they *do* something?" is the question most asked by young ones. They want their parents to do something about the behavior of the user. They watch their parents rant and rave and accomplish nothing. They are very frightened when there are physical fights between their brother or sister and their parents. They watch all the rotten things that happen and then see their parents do things to help the user, like going to the juvenile center in the middle of the night to get him, or giving him money after he has been angry and awful, or offering him ten dollars for a C on his report card when they are getting As and not getting ten cents for it, or just not trying to stop him from doing whatever he wants to do. It is all very confusing to siblings who are trying hard to be good and getting little or no recognition for it.

They feel a lot of anger toward the parents and toward the user. The anger often brings on feelings of guilt because co-dependents believe that they should not be angry at their parents. Families are supposed to love each other, and good children do not have ugly feelings toward their parents. They also believe that it is wrong to hate their brother or sister, and they feel guilty about those feelings too. They sometimes feel that they are the cause of the using. If there are fights before school, co-dependents blame themselves for the fights and feel that their sibling uses because of them. Because they do not talk about their feelings, they do not find out that other young people feel the same way, that it is okay to feel angry at their parents, that it is okay to feel disappointed in their parents, that it is okay to feel confused, that it is okay to feel hateful toward someone who treats you badly. They need to know that feelings are not good or bad. They have no control over their feelings. What they do about their feelings they can control, but not the feelings themselves.

Co-dependent siblings need to realize that if anyone else treated them the way their brother or sister treats them, they would feel the same way toward that person as they do toward their brother or sister. Being so caught up in reacting to the behavior of the user, parents tend to neglect the rest of the family. It is natural for the other children to be angry at their parents for not paying attention to them and for not doing anything about the behavior of the user. It is truly disappointing to see parents unable to deal with the acting-out behavior of a brother or sister. Since the whole family gets tangled up in the disease of chemical dependency, it is important for the whole family to get help to unsnarl the tangles.

Late Stage Co-dependency of Siblings

By the time the feelings of anger and extreme dislike are boiling in the co-dependent sibling, the disease is going into the late stage. Older siblings have usually found a way to leave home—

going to school, living on their own. Those who are still at home usually withdraw from the situation. Joy Jocque had stopped talking to her family about what was happening at school or with her friends. She spent as much time away from home as possible and went on with her life without including her parents in it, applying for and winning a scholarship to a school of her own choosing, thus being able to leave home. Kerrie Nile stayed as far from Dean as possible. Barry Vivial tried to avoid Connie when she was home and was relieved when she was not around. Sometimes the user torments a sibling who plays his game, and there is constant arguing and fighting when the two are together.

If the mother is a single mother, the nonusing sibling may try to protect her from the user. If the user is especially abusive, the smaller children may be very angry with their mother for not protecting them from the user. They do not realize that their mother feels as powerless over the user as they do.

By the time a young user is in the late stage of dependency, the family is in despair. No one in the house feels good. Everyone's self-esteem is low, and no one wants to be there. The whole family would like some magic genie to come and fix everything. Even though they have experienced disappointment again and again, the siblings of users still want their parents to make things better. They still think it is their parents' job to do something about the user, and they look to them to take steps to end what is happening in the family.

COPING WITH A DRUG-ABUSING SIBLING

No one can cope with a drug user alone. It is impossible to deal with the situation without help. A young person needs the guidance of adults and support from people who understand the problem. Al-Anon and Alateen are good places to find support. School counselors know what resources are available in your community. Many cities and counties have offices associated with the National Council on Alcoholism. The NCA has a list of community resources that help families. Today most alcoholism counselors are drug-abuse counselors as well, recognizing the disease as chemical dependency. The telephone yellow pages have listings of counselors under Alcoholism and under Drug

Abuse. Many resources are available to answer questions and to offer help.

If you have a brother or sister who is into drugs, it is extremely important that you do not cover for him or her. When you cover, you allow the disease to progress and to get a firmer hold on your sibling and your family. You enable the user to become more and more deeply involved. It is vital to your brother or sister and to your family that you let your parents know what is going on. You can be the one to start your family on the road to recovery.

If you cannot talk to your parents yourself, find someone to help you. If there is a Toughlove Parent Support Group in your community, suggest that your parents go to a meeting. Call the number for Toughlove and ask them to send some of their literature to your parents. Go to an Alateen meeting and meet other teens who are struggling with the same problems you are. Call the alcoholism treatment facility in your area and ask if they have groups for brothers and sisters of drug users. Some facilities have free support group meetings. Find help for yourself. You do not need to wait for your parents to do something.

If you have been covering for your sibling for a long time, it will be difficult to break that pattern. That is why support is so important. You will not be able to stop your enabling behavior without support from Alateen or a community support group. There may be a support group for family and friends of users in your school. Look for your support to stop enabling your brother or sister to use and your family to get sicker. Chemical dependency is a progressive disease, but the progression of the disease can be checked at any stage. You can be the one to help stop the deadly progression of the disease in your family.

CHAPTER IX

Coping with Friends Who Drink and Use Drugs

As he watched Stewart Stoner walk angrily away, Allen Average felt frustrated and sad. He and Stew had been friends since fourth grade, and he hated to see what was happening to him. They had drifted apart since junior high when Stew had started smoking pot and hanging around with the druggies at school. Allen had tried to stay friends with Stew, but it had been impossible. He still talked to him sometimes, but more and more it ended up like today. It seemed that the only time Stew looked Allen up was when he wanted to borrow money. At first Allen had lent Stew money when he needed it, and at first Stew had paid him back—or at least part of what he owed. Before long, however, Stew just forgot about paying, and finally Allen had stopped lending him money. That is what had made Stew so angry on this day. Allen felt bad about saying no, but he had promised himself that he would not lend Stew any more money.

Looking back on the last three years, Allen tried to figure out what he could have done to help Stew more. They had been such good friends that he hated to see it all go down the drain. Allen knew that Stew was doing a lot of drugs and had been for quite a while. In fact, that is what had driven him away from Stew in eighth grade. When Stew had first starting smoking pot in seventh grade with some of the older boys, Allen had tried it a few times too. But he did not like pot or Stew's new friends either, and he felt guilty about using it because he knew it was wrong. Stew had tried to get all their friends involved, but the only one who had gone along with him was Dean Nile, who was not really a close friend of Allen's. As Stew got more and more involved, Allen found other people to be with and other things to do. By eighth grade he was not seeing much of Stew because they were not in the same classes and Stew was cutting school a lot.

It was hard for Allen to let go of Stew completely. That is why he had continued to lend him money from time to time, but now he could not do that any longer. Allen was sad about the trouble his friend was getting into, but he no longer felt comfortable around Stew and because of Stew's reputation did not want anyone to associate him with Stew.

This was the third day in a row that Patti Pardee was waiting for Hannah Helper after school. When Hannah saw Patti, she sighed inwardly and wondered what disaster needed fixing today. She and Patti had been best friends since sixth grade and had told each other everything. Knowing everything about Patti was getting to be a pretty heavy load these days. Lately Patti had been asking Hannah to cover for her when she went out at night. Patti would tell her mother that she was at Hannah's house, and if Mrs. Pardee called, Hannah had agreed to tell her that Patti was in the bathroom or had gone down to the corner store for gum or something. Mrs. Pardee had not called, but Hannah was worried about what to say if she insisted that Patti call her back. Patti assured Hannah that her mother would just want to know that she was there.

Hannah was worried about Patti because of the crowd she was running around with. Patti told her all about the parties she was going to and how much fun it was to drink and get high. Hannah kept telling her to be careful and not to drink so much. Patti just laughed and told her to come along for some fun. Hannah figured that Patti was having more than enough fun for both of them and began to work on getting her involved in some other things. Patti would agree to go to the movies with her on Saturday night, and Hannah would be relieved until she found out that Patti had arranged to meet her party friends at the theater and then would take off with them after the show.

With all the cutting of classes, Patti's grades had started to drop, so Hannah had been helping her with her homework. Actually, Hannah had been doing Patti's homework, and she figured that was probably what Patti wanted today just as she had the past two days. The only reason Hannah did it was because she did not want Patti to get in trouble. Patti's parents were really rough on her about her grades and about most other things too. They had all kinds of rules and regulations that seemed unreasonable. Hannah could understand why Patti sneaked out so much. Lately they had been screaming at Patti and treating her horribly.

Ever since she had known Patti, Hannah had been there to listen and comfort her. She was glad that she was there for Patti because without her Patti would have had an even rougher time. Hannah knew that Patti really needed a friend, and she could not desert her when things were getting so bad. She was sure that if she tried hard enough she could get Patti to see how partying and cutting school were not going to make things better at home, so she would have to cover until Patti came to her senses.

Sue Saver and Bob Brink had been together for over a year, and Sue still felt lucky to have him for a boyfriend. He was sure of himself and did not care if anyone liked what he did or not. Sometimes that caused problems with other people, who accused him of being arrogant and cold. They just did not understand him the way Sue did. She knew that he was tough on the outside because he did not want anyone to know how sensitive he really was. Understanding Bob as she did, Sue knew that he really cared about her and depended on her. He was pretty quiet about his feelings, but Sue could look at him and see what kind of a mood he was in. She knew when to be careful and talkative and when to be quiet and give Bob time to work out whatever was bothering him. Keeping Bob happy was her major goal, and she spent most of her time figuring out how best to do that.

Part of keeping Bob happy was looking after him. Sue insisted that he do his homework when he came over in the evening, went to the library with him when he had to do research, reminded him about Mother's Day and Father's Day, worried about him when he was sick, scolded him when he did things that he should not. She knew that Bob just could not get along without her.

Only one thing worried Sue, and that was Bob's drinking. All of the kids in their crowd partied, but Bob was getting drunk almost every weekend. Sue had stopped drinking at all when they went out because she wanted to be able to drive home in case Bob had too much. The first time he had been angry that she thought he could not drive home, and she had given in. She was terrified all the way home, and the next day had told him how scared she was. Bob had forgotten yelling at her when she wanted to drive, and he apologized for not letting her. After that is was agreed that Sue would drive home from all parties.

At first Sue thought that the problem was taken care of, but as time went on and Bob got drunk every weekend, she began to worry about the drinking itself. She would watch how much he drank and try to get him to leave before he got drunk. She would try to divert his attention from drinking and get him to dance or talk to others who were not drinking so much. She had suggested that they do other things besides go to parties, but he said he wanted to be with his friends. Nothing seemed to work, and lately he had begun to ignore her at parties and tell her to leave him alone when she tried to get his attention away from the drinking. In fact, he had been hanging around Patti Pardee, whom Sue considered a real low-life, at the last two parties.

On the way home from the most recent party Sue mentioned how much he had been drinking lately, and Bob got really mad. He told her that she was jealous because she could not loosen up and have a good time. He accused her of trying to run his life and said he was tired of her acting like he was some sort of idiot who could not take care of himself. He yelled and swore at her, and she ended up in tears. Bob had almost pushed her out of the car when they got to her house and had roared off without saying goodnight. Sue was out of her mind all night, and when she called Bob the next day he did not remember anything that had happened on the way home. In fact, he thanked her for making sure that he got home okay.

Sue was very confused. Bob was so different when he drank, and he treated her so badly. She truly did not want to make him angry, but she wanted him to know how worried she was. She tried so hard to keep him from drinking too much at parties, but nothing she did made any difference. Now she was afraid to say anything about it for fear of making him angry. She wondered if she should tell him what really happened on the way home. Was he pretending not to remember because he wanted her to ignore it, or did he really not remember? Sue did not know what to think or what to do.

WHEN FRIENDS DRINK AND USE

Friends are for sharing and caring, for having fun and for being angry and making up, for doing something with or doing nothing with. Friends are there to cheer you up when you are feeling down or to shout with you when you are winning. Friends are for leaning on when you cannot stand alone. Some friends are special because they have been a part of your life for a long time, and others become very special in a short time.

It is natural when people you care about are in trouble to want to help them. When friends confide in you, it shows that they trust and respect you, and you feel needed and worthwhile in return. Part of the sharing in a friendship involves giving advice when you see friends doing harmful things to themselves and being confronted by them when you are headed in a wrong direction.

When friends begin to drink and use, natural sharing gets all confused. Feeling that they will get into trouble if adults find out, your first response is to cover for them. You want to talk to them and help them. Sometimes they will share what they are doing with you, but often they will only let you know what they want you to know so they can keep your support. They tell you how difficult things are and how adults do not understand them and give them a bad time. If things had not been going well with parents before, when regular use begins things really go downhill. Your using friend may come to you for the comfort and support you have always provided, as Patti did to Hannah. When she did not need Hannah, Patti was off with her new friends doing her thing.

It is very easy to get trapped on the merry-go-round of chemical dependency with a friend who comes for advice and comfort and help. Preserving the trusting relationship and confidentiality you have with your friend is so important that you try to handle the situation yourself, and the secrets you carry weigh you down and keep you from moving on with your own life. You become so involved with covering for your friend or trying to help him see what he is doing to himself that you neglect your own needs. Hannah was so focused on Patti that she compromised her own values in her efforts to rescue Patti. With that compromising of values, Hannah put the seal on her co-dependency and was caught in the trap of addiction. The more she "helped" Patti, the more she enabled Patti to continue her destructive behavior. Being a good friend to Patti was putting them both deeper and deeper into addiction and co-addiction.

It is not unusual for girls to involve themselves with boys in addictive type relationships. They focus all their attention on pleasing their boyfriend, dropping girls who have been longtime friends to be with their boyfriend. They will make all their time available to their boyfriend and give up things they like to do or do things they do not particularly enjoy just to be with him. Girls usually do this because they think that their role as girlfriend requires sacrificing all for the relationship, that it proves how much they care about the boy, that he will then realize how important they are to him and return their devotion.

Sue Saver was Bob Brink's caretaker and chief enabler. As soon as Sue began going with Bob she started her campaign to make herself indispensable to him. When his drinking began to bother her, she did not try to find help for him; she tried to *be* the help for him. The harder she tried to make things better, the more harmfully involved with alcohol she and Bob became, and the harder she had to try to make the relationship work. Even though Sue was not drinking, she was just as involved with alcohol as Bob because his use was dictating her behavior. She began to focus on how much he was drinking and how drunk he was or might become.

Co-dependency had a firm hold on Sue because everything she did was aimed at making Bob change—when he did not want to do his schoolwork, she made sure he did the research at the library and got his homework done; when he drank too much she tried to get him to cut down or do other things. She took responsibility for and managed the consequences of his behavior, or at least she tried to.

CO-DEPENDENCY OF FRIENDS OF USERS

Society urges you to help others. You are taught that it is good to think of others first. Song lyrics tell you that loving someone means being everything and giving everything to that person. The focus of your being is supposed to be outside of yourself. Being the helper, the saver, the one others can depend on can set you up for a dependent relationship. Once you put yourself in the position of someone who manages things or fixes and makes better, it is easy to get caught on the merry-go-round of chemical dependency. You take on problems that require more wisdom and experience than you have, and you never think to ask for help because you have always been the one that others looked to for help. It never occurs to you that helping someone who is drinking and using requires special knowledge and expertise that you do not have. And once you are on the merry-go-round, it is very difficult to get off because it usually means giving up the relationship.

Allen Average almost got caught in dependency first and co-dependency later. His choice not to use and become involved with drugs cost him the relationship with Stew. It was difficult to let go completely, so Allen kept Stew's secret, and when he lent Stew money he knew what Stew was going to use it for and that he would not get it back. It took Allen three years to finally close the door on the relationship, and then it was with sadness. Co-dependency was there, tugging at him to continue the contact with Stew and maybe help him.

Because it feels good when you help others is another reason it is so easy to get caught on the merry-go-round. If you are always willing to help others and seldom ask for help yourself, you are a prime candidate for co-dependency. That does not mean that you should never help others, but it does mean that you need be aware that you are the kind of person who may take on more than you can handle. If you have friends whose alcohol and/or drug use is a concern to you, do not try to solve that problem for them. They need professional help. By trying to help them yourself, you become as harmfully involved as they are, and your co-dependency becomes as big a problem as their dependency.

HELPING FRIENDS WHO DRINK AND USE

When you are concerned about the drinking and using of friends, always remember that YOU CANNOT HELP THEM BY YOURSELF. The best way you can help is to get them to people who have the knowledge and expertise to help them. In other words, you must become a part of a referral system, and that means you must do some research to find out what kind of effective help is available to you and your friends.

Begin by checking at school. If there is a special chemical dependency counselor, make an appointment to talk to him or her immediately. The chemical dependency counselor is usually not one of the regular counselors but someone who works only with students with chemical problems.

If your school has a coordinator or director of drug and alcohol programs, call and find out what programs are available in your school and community. Knowing the resources in the community is an important part of the job of any coordinator of drug programs.

Some schools have support groups for people concerned about the use of friends or relatives. Your counselor would know if such a group is available. Concerned persons support groups help you to work through your fears and feelings of inadequacy in dealing with users. They offer support when tough decisions must be made. Being with other students who are coping with the same problems and feelings makes it easier because you know you are not alone.

Many times school nurses are good people to contact because they know the resources in the community. They can help you find the best place to get help for yourself and your friends.

Regular school counselors may know what resources are in your community as well as in your school. They may have a special interest in chemical dependency, and talking to them may help you to deal with your feelings about your friends. They may be able to talk to your friends and refer them to the help they need.

Some science, health, and physical education teachers take a special interest in drug and alcohol abuse and make it a point to

know what help is available at school and in the community. If
you feel comfortable with them and trust them, they can be very
helpful in getting you to the help you need.

Because you may not want to put your friends in a bad spot,
you may not want to do your school research in person. The
telephone is a wonderful, anonymous tool. You can call people
and ask questions without having to reveal your identity.

County or state health services can give you information and
refer you to services that are available in your community. If
there is a teen clinic, teen hot-line, drug hot-line, or alcohol and
drug program, call and talk with someone about your concerns.

The branch of the National Council on Alcoholism in your
city has a resource list of counselors and agencies. There are
often counselors in the office who will talk with you and assist
you in finding the services that best suit your needs. They will
definitely refer you to Al-Anon and Alateen and may even help
you find a meeting you can attend. Help is as near as your
phone.

RECOGNIZING HELPFUL PEOPLE

Talking to an adult about something as important as a friend's
alcohol and drug use is very difficult, and deciding whether the
person can be trusted requires careful thought. A few guidelines
will help you determine if the person you talk to is one you can
feel confident will help you and your friends who are using.

Are you treated in a nonjudgmental way?

When you talk to someone at school, you need to feel that
what you tell is accepted and not judged. If the person you
confide in makes remarks that cause you to feel guilty or wrong,
that make you want to defend your using friends, that let you
know the adult disapproves of you or your friends, you will not
get the help you need from that person.

In addition to having an adult involved in helping your
friends, it is important that you feel you are being offered support and guidance. In a concerned and caring way, you need to
be helped to determine what resources and options are available
to you. A knowledgeable adult knows that you need support to
take care of your own needs and will refer you to that support.

Is there confidentiality?

It is important that what you discuss with the adult helper be held in strictest confidence. If the person wants you to name names so that parents can be called, you are not with a truly helping person. It is not always appropriate to call parents immediately. The helping person needs to talk with your friends to get some idea of what is going on with them. While talking with them, family situations can be discussed. If further investigation is warranted, the helper can do some checking. The determination of when and how to inform parents is very important and can make the difference as to whether or not your friends accept help.

You must feel free to talk without fear that what you say will get to someone who may be hurt or who may hurt you. Because of the fear of being considered a narc, it takes a lot of courage to talk to an adult about friends who use. It would be disastrous to you and totally unethical of the adult if your friends found out prematurely that you had talked to someone about their using. There is an appropriate time for your friends to find out about your concern, but only after you have given permission to release the information.

Is there a referral system?

When you do your research at school, ask the person you talk to what the process is for referring students to help for drug problems. If there is no system, there is probably little or no effective help. If you are not personally referred to help for yourself, there is something missing. You may not be able to get help for your friends, but you certainly can expect to receive support for yourself.

Find out how long it takes from the time of referral to the time someone contacts the person referred. If it takes longer than a day or two, it is too long. The willingness to talk to someone may very well be gone by the time someone gets around to making the contact.

Sometimes school personnel who have no training in chemical dependency try to counsel users. They genuinely want to help and feel that the user just needs someone who cares and understands; however, they usually end up with the user either refusing to cooperate or completely conning them. When chemically dependent young people get to competent help, they often trade "war stories" about how they conned school counselors who knew nothing about addiction. If you feel you know more about addiction then the counselor you are talking to, that is not a person who can help you or your friends. Trust the person who is a supportive, nonjudgmental listener and who refers you to a chemical dependency specialist and self-help groups in your community.

What if you cannot get help for your friends?

If you cannot help your friends, at least get help for yourself. Find a person or a group to give you the support you need so that you will not become a Hannah Helper or a Sue Saver or a Felix Fixer. Keep in mind the following behaviors that enable using to continue and put you on the merry-go-round of dependency and co-dependency.

Do not sympathize with using friends when they tell sad stories of how everyone is making life miserable for them. They want you to see them as victims and rescue them. When they start to complain, say, "It sounds like you could use some help. Mr. Counselor could help you." They will make excuses about why they cannot see Mr. Counselor and why you should do what they want instead. Do not let that bother you; just repeat, "You need help and Mr. Counselor could help you." Whatever they say, keep repeating that they need to see Mr. Counselor. That will keep you out of the rescuer-saver-fixer role.

Do not rescue your friends from the consequences of their behavior. Some of the rescuing and enabling things they may ask you to do are to lend them money, give them your homework to copy, tell their parents they were with you, give them a place to stay when they run away, give them food when they run away, buy their lunch when they spend their lunch money on drugs, side with them when they are rude and defiant toward adults, lie for them, give them rides when their parents will not.

Do not try to control the drinking or using. It will not do any good and may make them angry enough to strike out at you. Instead, find help for yourself and try to get them referred to help.

Do not take responsibility for their using. You may think that if you tried harder to understand them, they would stop using. Perhaps you feel that arguing with them or refusing to give them your homework upset them so much that they used. They will use whether you argue with them or not, so stop taking responsibility.

Do not see your using friends as being incapable of taking care of themselves. Sue thought it was her job to see that Bob did his homework and insisted that he go to the library when he had a paper to write. By her very actions she told him that he was incompetent, a loser. Her efforts to take charge and make his life wonderful sent the message that he was not handling his responsibilities; therefore, he was not a capable person.

Do not get trapped into thinking that you are the only one who can help your friends. Being there for Patti when she was needed made Hannah a prisoner. She was so intent on saving Patti that she gave up her freedom. Hannah dropped whatever she was doing when Patti wanted her and was left by herself when Patti was too busy for her. Yet Hannah felt obligated to cover for Patti as long as she felt she could help her, and she was sure that if she tried hard enough she could help. The belief that you can help will make you helpless. Anytime you feel you are the best one to help someone, RUN for help yourself!

When friends begin to get into trouble with alcohol and other drugs and you want to do something about it, there is one major thing to remember. There is help at school or in your community, and you need that help because YOU CANNOT HANDLE IT ALONE!

CHAPTER X

Coping with Your Own Chemical Use

As he stood on the sidewalk watching Fran Friendly drive off with another couple, Vernon Verge felt confused and defeated. Shoulders hunched over, head down, arms dangling at his sides, Vern looked as though someone had let the air out of him. Fran had not answered his calls on Sunday and had avoided him all day at school, and when he had finally managed to get her to talk to him, she had said she could not believe he had the nerve to speak to her after what happened Saturday night. With that she had stormed off and gotten in the car with Greg Garious and Kay Kind. Vern felt scared as well as confused because he did not remember what had happened on Saturday night, but he did know that Fran was disgusted with him because he had been drunk and stoned. He had promised himself that he would not get drunk because Fran had threatened to break up with him if he got drunk when he was with her. He was only going to have one glass of beer and sip it slowly all night, but once he had the beer in his hand, it was gone before he knew what had happened and was refilled without his asking. There was lots of marijuana around, and Vern could dimly remember someone offering him some crank, but he was so out of it that he was not sure. He did not know how he got home or how Fran got home. What he did know was that he had lost his girlfriend, and he had to face the fact that it was because he had been drunk once too often.

Vern did not know what to do. He felt as though he were an outsider watching his life fall apart, completely helpless to do anything about it. When Fran had told him she would break up with him if he got drunk again, she had also told him what he said and how he acted when he was drunk. Vern could not believe he could do and say those things when he cared about her so much. He had never felt about a girl the way he felt about Fran. He must have done something really bad on Saturday, and since Greg and Kay had been angry, he knew he must have done something to offend them too. What a mess!

As he turned to go back to his locker, Vern saw his counselor, Mr. Shepherd, going into his office. Two years ago when Vern had been having a hard time at home he had talked to Mr. Shepherd, and it had helped him a lot. Seeing the counselor made Vern think that maybe talking to him was what he needed now. Following Mr. Shepherd to his office, Vern asked if they could talk for just a minute. After listening to Vern, Mr. Shepherd said very simply, "You're worried about your alcohol and drug use." Vern, with a bleak look in his eyes, just nodded.

Handing Vern a survey sheet that Melanie Mender had left with him when she had visited the school a few weeks before, Mr. Shepherd suggested that Vern spend a few minutes doing it for his own information. As Vern read the questions he sighed. When he looked up, he said, "I need help."

Mr. Shepherd recommended that Vern see a drug and alcohol counselor for an evaluation. Since there was no one qualified on the counseling staff at school, he suggested that Vern see someone outside. It would mean having his parents involved, so Mr. Shepherd asked Vern how he wanted to handle that. Knowing that his parents would have to know sooner or later, Vern asked Mr. Shepherd to help him tell them, so they arranged a conference for a few days later. Mr. Shepherd told the Verges that it concerned a very confidential matter and it would be best if they did not question Vernon about it. As a result, Vern did not have any difficult questions from his parents before the conference.

As expected, Mr. and Mrs. Verge were very upset, but with Mr. Shepherd's help they realized that Vern needed help and their support, so they accepted Mr. Shepherd's offer to call a drug and alcohol abuse counselor and give the background of what had happened to that point. The Verges talked very briefly with the addiction counselor and made an appointment to get an evaluation of Vern's chemical use. When they left the office, the three Verges were committed to getting help for their family.

Penny Pardee was Patti's younger sister. When Patti began causing trouble at home, she began getting all the attention from their parents. Penny tried very hard to be good so her parents would notice her, but no matter what she did, they seemed not to appreciate it. Patti kept telling Penny what a great time she was having, and Penny felt it was very unfair. After school Patti brought friends over when their parents were not home, and Penny did not like what was going on; however, she was afraid to say anything to their parents because Patti told her that she had better keep her mouth shut.

Almost every day Patti or one of her friends would try to get Penny to "just take one hit" off a joint, and she resisted as long as she could. Finally, Penny did take a hit, and everybody cheered. They made a big deal about how she was finally getting smart, and Patti acted really proud that her little sister was getting high with them. After that, Penny began to dress differently, wear more makeup, and act "tough." At school she attracted more attention from the kids who were rowdy and used drugs. She cut a few classes, made some smart remarks to teachers, and did not do her homework. Some of her grades went down a little, and her mother told her to get to work and bring them up. Her father made a passing comment about how much makeup she was using, but other than that neither parent seemed to notice her much. Patti was so out of hand that Penny could not be bad enough for her parents to notice. That is, until "the Incident" at school.

One day Penny and her friends were in the restroom smoking a joint between classes when a teacher who had smelled something funny walked in and caught them. Taken to the principal's office, they were suspended for three days, and their parents were called to come and get them. Penny was so scared and embarrassed that she wanted to die. The only thing her mother said when she arrived was, "Not you too." When her father got home and heard the news, he just looked at her bleakly and shook his head. It was as though both of her parents had given up.

When the three-day suspension was up and Penny went back to school, she had little makeup on, was wearing very "straight" clothes, and tried to be as unnoticeable as possible. She avoided her new friends and stayed with Karen Konstant as much as possible. She had called Karen while she was on suspension and was relieved and happy to find that Karen still would be her friend.

From that point on, Penny decided to stay clean and get good grades. Maybe her parents would notice her and appreciate her, but if they did not, she would still do what she knew was best because she owed it to herself. She became involved in school activities and avoided Patti and her friends by not being around when they were at the house. She had come too close to being like them. The humiliation of being suspended for marijuana possession was enough to make Penny take a good look at where she was going and to realize that she did not want to go down that road.

The same thought spun round and round in Mark Margin's head, "How did I get into this mess?" He was sitting in Mr. Shepherd's office waiting to hear that he would not earn all of his credits for this year if his grades did not come up immediately. He knew that was why he had been called in, but what Mark wanted to do was to tell Mr. Shepherd how miserable he felt. And somehow or other as soon as they started talking, that is exactly what he did.

Things had been going badly for Mark since school started in September. He could not seem to get interested in his classes this year. All of the guys he ran around with now were not into school, and it was hard for Mark to stay in class when the other guys were out having fun. Actually, what they were doing was drinking beer and smoking dope and snorting a little crank once in a while. Last summer Mark had really got into smoking pot pretty heavily. He had played with it before, but last summer he had been out at the lake with the guys almost every day drinking beer and smoking pot.

When school started Mark had cut classes a few times, but his folks found out and threw such a fit that he decided it was not worth cutting if he had to put up with that. He went to class every day, but he did not do his homework or study for tests. When report cards came out, he was in hot water again. When he began coming home late for dinner, his parents made a criminal offense of it. They wanted to treat him like a baby and not let him out of their sight for a minute. What began as a small battle ended up as all-out war. Now Mark could not come in the door without being yelled at. He was constantly fighting with his parents and dreaded being around them for even a minute. He used to get along real well with his folks, and now he almost hated them.

Some of his old friends were avoiding him now. He would not have minded that so much if he had not overheard a girl he liked a lot say to another girl, "It's too bad Mark is getting to be such a scumbag. He's hanging out with a bunch of burnouts and looks like he hasn't showered in weeks. Yeah, it's sure too bad; I used to think a lot of him." Mark had not considered himself scummy-looking, but when he took a good look he could see that he was not too clean and his clothes were getting ragged.

Mark might have been more defensive about his appearance and his friends if Saturday night had not happened. They were all out drinking and smoking dope and snorting a little crank as usual when Sonny Savage decided it would be fun to light the tail of a cat with his lighter. Mark could not get the sound of the cat's yowling out of his head. Everybody was so loaded that they all laughed; but Mark left early and on the way home he kept throwing up until he was lying on somebody's lawn too weak to move. When he could finally sit up, he vowed that he would never go out with those dudes again. He wanted no more to do with people who could be so brutal. He may have dropped low, but he was not that low.

And here he was two weeks later, pouring out the whole mess to Mr. Shepherd. Mark had not used or had anything to drink since that night, and he had no intention of using again. Mr. Shepherd offered to help Mark in any way he could. He suggested that Mark go to the Young People's Alcoholics Anonymous meeting on Thursday night and gave him the telephone number of a boy he knew named Jerry who went to that meeting.

It had taken all the courage Mark had to dial the phone number that Mr. Shepherd had given him, and he was feeling anxious and scared when he walked into the meeting with Jerry. Because everyone was so friendly and two guys who knew him from school came up and welcomed him to the meeting, it did not take Mark long to relax and listen to what was being said. As people told their stories and shared their feelings, Mark began to feel that he was not alone, that there were lots of young people just like him who did not want to continue drinking and using and ruining their lives.

LOOKING AT YOUR OWN DRUG/ALCOHOL USE

It is difficult to admit to yourself that you are in trouble with drugs and alcohol. Most young people are convinced that they "can handle it." It usually takes something jolting to break through that denial—Vern had to lose a girlfriend, Penny had to be humiliated, and Mark had to feel sick about the cruelty of his buddies—but the signs of trouble are there long before the jolting event.

Penny was the least involved of all, but there were some early trouble signs. She liked being accepted by her sister's friends, began dressing like them, and soon was accepted by the rowdy crowd at school. To stay "in" with that group, she had to act hard and be a disturbance in school—no big deal, but enough to be noticed. As a result of her new attitude toward school, her grades went down; again, no big deal, but enough to be noticeable. Then came the suspension for possession, the bolt of lightning that hit her hard enough to turn her around. So for Penny the early indicators that her drug use was getting out of hand were the changes in dress, friends, and attitude toward school.

The same indicators of trouble were there for Mark, but they had reached a more critical point because of his longer and heavier use. Mark was looking really scroungy, and his friends were heavy-duty users who no longer cared about anything but drinking and using. Even though he got his body to school every day, his brain was so full of THC from marijuana that he could not concentrate or remember anything anyway, so he was in danger of failing. At home things were so bad that Mark wanted to leave, and it is a good bet that his parents wished he would! He could still feel sad about the loss of his good relationship with his parents, and he did go to school because they demanded it. He was not into his dependency to the point of not caring about his parents. Mark's trouble signs were lack of care for his personal appearance, failing grades at school, friends with "Don't-care-itis," and fighting and unhappiness at home.

Because of the sick incident with the cat, Mark's defense system was weakened, and when he overheard the comments by a girl he respected he knew that he had to do something. Being called in to see Mr. Shepherd gave him the opportunity to reach for the help he needed, and he found support and friends at AA.

The love affair with alcohol that Vern was having was much like that of thousands of young people who party only on weekends. Because he did not drink alone and did not drink every day, he thought he did not have a problem, but he was experiencing some serious consequences of drinking. Vern was a different person when he drank; his personality changed. He was getting enough feedback from Fran to know that he had to cut down, so he promised himself that he would not get drunk and got drunk anyway, making him feel ashamed of himself. He was having blackouts, and that made him feel anxious and guilty and scared. Fran's complete disgust and refusal to have any more to do with him gave Vern the jolt he needed to ask for help. His serious warning signs were the personality change when he drank, getting drunk when he did not mean to, blackouts, and feelings of guilt, shame, anxiety, and fear.

Like Mark, Vern, and Penny, you can stop using before it is out of control. If you are reading this and are concerned about your own use, you are ready to be honest with yourself and look at your chemical use. Chapter VI, Chemically Dependent Teens, gives you a good description of the stages of dependency. The following survey, similar to the one Vern filled out in Mr. Shepherd's office, gives you an opportunity to look at your own use.

CHEMICAL USE QUESTIONNAIRE*

yes   no   1. Do you lose time from school because of drinking or drug use?

yes   no   2. Do you think the more popular kids drink and use drugs?

yes   no   3. Do you consider yourself a person who drinks and uses drugs?

yes   no   4. Do you drink or use drugs to escape from study or home worries?

yes   no   5. Does it bother you if someone says maybe you drink too much or use too many drugs?

yes   no   6. Do you have to take a drink or use drugs because it makes you feel more comfortable on a date?

yes   no   7. Do you ever get into money trouble over buying liquor or drugs?

yes   no   8. Have you lost friends since you started drinking and using drugs?

yes   no   9. Do you hang out now with a crowd where stuff is easy to get?

yes   no   10. Have you ever gotten into trouble at home because of alcohol or drugs?

yes   no   11. Do you drink until the bottle is empty or until the drugs are gone?

yes   no   12. Have you ever had a loss of memory from drinking or taking drugs?

yes   no   13. Has driving under the influence ever put you in a hospital or jail?

yes   no   14. Do you get annoyed with classes or lectures on drugs or drinking?

yes   no   15. Do you sometimes hang out with kids who drink or use drugs?

yes   no   16. Do you use drugs or alcohol because it helps cheer you up when you are in a bad mood?

yes   no   17. Do you use drugs or alcohol to change the way you feel?

yes   no   18. Do you ever have times when you can't remember some of what happened while drinking or using drugs?

yes   no   19. Do you sometimes get drunk or loaded when you didn't start out to get that way?

yes   no   20. Do you think you have a problem with liquor or drugs?

---

*From *Young Alcoholics* (c) 1978, by Tom Alibrandi, published by CompCare Publications, Minneapolis, MN 55441; (800) 328-3330. Used by permission.

Every "yes" answer is a warning of a problem. If you answered "yes" to more than three questions, you need help. If you do not feel you can go to your parents, see a counselor or school nurse or another adult you feel you can trust. Call Alcoholics Anonymous and ask where and when you can attend a young people's AA meeting. Call the National Council on Alcoholism and ask for a referral to a counselor. Look in the telephone yellow pages under Alcoholism and Drug Abuse. Look in the white pages under County Health Services for drug and alcohol services. Find out if there is a teen clinic to refer you to a counselor. Look on the bulletin board in the nurse's office or a counselor's office at school.

There are many places for you to go for help, but do not try to handle it by yourself. You need the support of caring adults, and you can find them. Give your parents the first chance to help you. If you need support to tell them that you are having problems with drugs, get an adult you trust to support you when you talk to your parents.

Do not wait until tomorrow or next week. Do not try to be strong and do it by yourself. You need support and you need it right now, today. Your community has the people and the resources to help you. Drugs and alcohol will not let go of you easily. You need all the help you can get. The time to begin recovery is now.

CHAPTER XI

Chemical Dependency and You

Coping with chemical dependency is a tall order. If you live in a family with an active user of chemicals, you live in an unpredictable world where reality is denied. You have learned the rules of Don't Talk, Don't Trust, Don't Feel. Not until you break those rules can you and your family get help, so DO talk about the use and the behavior of the chemical abuser; DO trust others to help you find the help *you* need for yourself first and for your family second; DO feel your fear, anxiety, anger, frustration, love, anguish, caring, joy, helplessness, and powerlessness and allow them to move you to get help for yourself and your family.

You do not have to feel ashamed or helpless because you live in a family with a chemically dependent person. You do not have to feel guilty if you are chemically dependent yourself. You and your family are dealing with a disease that is much like any other treatable chronic disease. You now know where to get help, and you know that helping professionals who understand the family disease of chemical dependency do not see alcoholism and addiction as symptoms of some underlying emotional problem but recognize chemical dependency as a primary disease.

A LAST LOOK AT CO-DEPENDENCY

You may not drink or use drugs yourself or live in a family with a chemically dependent person, but look at your behavior and see if you have the characteristics of a co-dependent.

- Do you worry about someone's behavior—how much they drink or use or how they behave; what other people would think of you if they knew about that person's behavior?

- Do you worry about how someone feels and take responsibility for the way they feel? If your girlfriend is unhappy, do you think you are to blame? If your father is angry, do you think it is your fault? When it is raining and your boyfriend is mad because he cannot go fishing, do you feel guilty?

- Do you make excuses for someone's behavior? He drinks because he has a high-stress job. She needs to take Valium because my brother is hyperactive. He drinks only when things are bad at home.

- Do you feel as though another person cannot manage without you? Do you feel you are the only one who understands? Your girlfriend tells you that you are the only one she can trust. Your mother needs you to keep the family together. Your boyfriend does not drink too much when you are with him. Your boyfriend does his homework because you insist on it. Your parents stop fighting when you intervene.

- Do you lie for others to keep them out of trouble? Do you lie to cover for a friend whose mother might be upset if she knew where the friend really was? Have you told someone that your mother was sick when she was drunk or hung over? Have you told your parents your sister cleaned the house when you were the one who did it so you would not have to listen to them fight?

- Do you lie to yourself so you will not feel the pain, anxiety, fear, and loneliness of living in a chemically dependent home or being involved with a chemically dependent person?

- Do you try to please others to make them happy; to keep them from being angry; so they will like you; so they will pay attention to you?

- Do you try to manage things so everything will be all right? Do you take responsibility for the younger children and see that they behave and are clean and cared for? Do you try to keep dinner conversation on a safe subject? Do you watch your boyfriend at a party and try to divert his attention so he does not drink too much? When you are out with another couple, do you feel it is your responsibility to keep the conversation moving and to make everyone feel good?

• Are you so busy taking care of everyone else and worrying about how they feel that you do not know what your own feelings are? Do you ever tell yourself, "I shouldn't feel that way," and then work hard *not* to feel that way?

• Do you do what others want and neglect what you would like to do? Are you always doing favors for others so that you do not have time for yourself?

• Are you afraid that something bad will happen if you are not there to take care of things? Do you feel something terrible might happen to your friend if you are not there to listen? Are you afraid that the fights at home will be worse if you are not there?

• Do you think it is wonderful to be needed by others and spend much of your time solving problems for other people?

If you answered "yes" to any of those questions, you have definite signs of co-dependency, and you need help for yourself. Go to Alateen or Al-Anon. Let your friends and relations take care of their own problems while you find constructive ways to help them as Joan Swig did for herself and her family.

PART OF THE PROBLEM OR PART OF THE SOLUTION?

Chemical dependency affects the minds and hearts of the people around the chemical abuser as well the alcoholic/addict. It is a vicious disease that is destroying millions of lives all over the world, but you can do something to stop its destruction. You may not be able to influence anyone else, but you can stop it in yourself right now. You can refuse to continue following the rules that keep you helpless, and you can get into a program of recovery for yourself. It may seem selfish to think of yourself first, but no one in your family will recover unless *someone* starts the process. You have read this book and have begun your education about the disease of chemical dependency. It is up to you to be a leader and share your knowledge with others. Become a part of the solution, for if you are not part of the solution, you are part of the problem.

CHAPTER XII

Substance Abuse in the 1990s

Chemical dependency is much more than a personal problem or a family problem or a community problem. It's a world problem. Because so much money is to be made in illegal drug trafficking, it has become big business, a gigantic worldwide corporation with countless smaller "companies," "branches," "subsidiaries," "silent partners," and "stockholders." This corporation touches the lives of almost every person in the world. It makes partners of a Maya farmer in Central America and a teenage gang member in Los Angeles. The teenager says he's not interested in going to school or getting a job because he makes a thousand dollars a day dealing drugs on the street. The Maya farmer plants marijuana where he once grew rice because his rice brings him 21 cents a pound and he gets $20 a pound for the marijuana.

Between 1981 and 1988 the U.S. government spent over $20 billion fighting the war against drugs, mainly trying to stop the flow of drugs into the country and out to the user. Laws were strengthened and personnel and training in law enforcement agencies increased. Much was spent on interdiction activities in Central and South America and the Caribbean and other places around the globe. Interdiction includes sending agents to find out who is behind the drug trade; where the marijuana, coca for cocaine, or opium poppies grow; how the U.S. can work with the power holders in the country to somehow intervene in the growing, processing, or shipping of the crop. It also means providing money to set up law enforcement activities in the countries. One Central American country has been lent two specially equipped, armored planes for spraying marijuana crops. These planes can fly very low over heavily guarded plantations without fear of harm from shots fired from the ground.

Billions of dollars are being spent in the Caribbean to intercept boats and planes running marijuana, cocaine, and crack from Colombia, Jamaica, and the Bahamas into Florida. Fifty-eight separate offices involving the Coast Guard, Customs, and the Drug Enforcement Administration use aircraft, boats, radar balloons, and agents along our southern borders and coasts where drugs come into the country.

Government agencies are working with farmers to show them how to grow food crops profitably so they won't have to grow marijuana and coca to feed their families. It's a difficult job when the farmer says that he'll be glad to plant corn as soon as he is guaranteed the same price he gets for his coca.

After years of focusing on interdiction, the government realized that little headway was being made. No matter how many drug runners they arrested or how much of the illegal cargo was confiscated, drugs still poured into the country. The supply side was only half of the problem. The demand side had to be attacked as well. Education for prevention and treatment for drug users is receiving attention. In October, 1988, Congress passed a bill providing $2.6 billion dollars to be spent over two years and stipulating that by the second year 60 percent of the funding must be spent on drug-abuse prevention and treatment.

Today more money is being spent within our borders on prevention and treatment. Worldwide, there is more interest in prevention. Producer nations are consumer nations and are experiencing the problems that go with drug use. U.S. government agencies in foreign countries are working with local governments to develop drug-prevention programs.

All of these activities are aimed at reducing U.S. problems that result from drug addiction. That is a lot of money, time, and energy spent because a relatively few people in the country want to get high and stay high. Why all the fuss?

CRIME

When asked how they got money for drugs, the unanimous reply from a group of recovering teenage addicts was,

"Stealin' and dealin'." One boy told how he "did houses," another got things at "five–finger discount" (shoplifting), a third mugged old people, a fourth stole hubcaps and radios from cars, still another stole the whole car. They all knew people who had held up stores.

Crime statistics all over the country have gone up as a result of drugs in the community. Murder rates have skyrocketed because of drug wars. Since 1985 when crack cocaine came to Washington, DC, the murder rate has gone from 148 per year to 372. Most of those were cases of drug dealers killing other dealers. Some 45,000 arrests were made as a result of sweeps through the known crack "bazaars" in the city without making a dent in the drug trade or the murder rate for two and a half years. Then in the spring of 1989 a big drug dealer in Washington was arrested. He had developed a family business that was believed to supply 20 percent of the coke used in the Washington area. Within two months of his arrest, police told *Newsweek* magazine, the murder rate had dropped 25 percent. Unfortunately, they expected someone else to show up to take over his territory.

Drug wars between gangs and dealers mean that dealers and gang members get killed. So who cares? It wouldn't matter so much if that's all there were to it. Unfortunately, "drug warriors" don't care who is in the way when they go after a target. Drive-by shootings where anyone in the way gets shot are not unusual. In Boston in August, 1988, Darlene Tiffany Moore was sitting on a mailbox talking to friends when a car drove past and sprayed the neighborhood with bullets. It was thought that the gunmen were after a neighbor who was dealing drugs. That didn't make Tiffany any less dead.

The Los Angeles gangs that are carrying on the drug wars there are expanding operations. They're taking their drug-dealing and killing to Kansas City, Tulsa, Omaha, Denver, St. Louis, and forty other cities. The Crips and the Bloods are bringing gangland mayhem to Middle America.

Rural America says, "Boy, I'm sure glad I don't live in the city." In March, 1989, a drug lab in Willow Springs, Missouri, in the Ozarks, was raided and twenty-five pounds of methamphetamine, a form of speed called "crank," was found. It had been "cooked" in the lab and had a street value of $1 million. Some people call crank the poor man's cocaine. Crank dealers are operating all over rural America, running farms or holding down regular jobs to cover their illegal drug-making activities. Crank "looms as a potential national drug crisis in the 1990s," predicts the National Institute on Drug Abuse.

Crack cocaine is no stranger to the small towns of America. In Burke County, Georgia, 100 crack dealers were arrested in a year's time. In the South, authorities think that rural drug rings will take over the trade. Small-town operators already supply the cities of North Carolina. The rural dealers go down to the remote areas of Florida to meet the planes from Jamaica and Colombia and make their buys directly from the suppliers.

Burglaries, robberies, and violent crime rates are going up in rural areas. As drug dealers come in, the violent crime rate goes up. Police chiefs and county sheriffs from Small Town, America, are concerned. There are no safe corners anymore.

The strain on law enforcement is getting worse as the drug gangs arm themselves with military-style assault weapons, machine guns, and fully automatic pistols. Many police departments now require their officers to wear bulky bullet-proof vests. Police are taught how to break into crack houses with one man holding a bulletproof shield in front of another man who batters down the door. Many are replacing their five-shot .38 pistols with new seventeen-shot 9-mm semi-automatics similar to the ones used by the gangs. The mental stress is so great that police departments across the country are providing stress-management programs for their officers. The psychological costs of the drug war are high.

BUSINESS AND POLITICS

Drug trafficking is big business. One of the biggest businesses in the world is run by the cocaine cartel in Colombia. A dozen families control 70 percent of the world's cocaine trade and make billions every year. Most of that money finds its way back to Colombia through a process of corruption called "money laundering."

One example of money laundering is that of a Colombian coffee trading and export/import firm that had offices on Wall Street in New York. Cash was brought from all over the U.S. and deposited by the firm in eighteen different bank accounts. By law, deposits of over $10,000 in currency must be reported. The Colombian company falsified the reports, and the money was deposited in accounts that were actually to dummy Panamanian corporations that existed only on paper. The deposits appeared legitimate and were available for withdrawal.

Once the money was safely deposited in the banks, it was transferred by wire directly to accounts in Panama banks. The money was then untraceable—laundered. It was returned to the cartel in the form of loans or investments or deposited directly to their bank accounts in Bogotá, Colombia.

In the money-laundering process, it is often necessary to pay off bank officials who know where huge sums of cash must be coming from. Officials in several banks in Florida have been convicted of money-laundering activities.

Government officials in Central and South America have been paid huge amounts to look the other way as drugs go out through their countries and money being laundered comes in.

In June, 1989, the Cuban government charged General Arnaldo Ochoa Sanchez of Cuba with money laundering, black marketing, drug trafficking, and treason. Five other officers were arrested two days later. The official Cuban newspaper *Granma* reported that Cubans charged Colombians from the cartel from $800 to $1,200 per kilogram of cocaine to move it safely through Cuba. Boats sent from Miami anchored in Varadero, a well-known Cuban resort, where the drugs were brought aboard for shipment to Florida. Planes belonging to Colombian drug runners were given identification codes that gave them safe passage over Cuba and allowed them to land in case of emergency. Cuban authorities were paid off in U.S. dollars. General Ochoa was executed in July.

General Manuel Antonio Noriega of Panama has been indicted in Florida for taking payoffs from the Colombian cocaine cartel in exchange for a clear corridor for drug traffickers through Panama. In early 1989 he and a small group of men opened a new bank in Panama called the Institutional Bank of the Fatherland. The bank opened with more than $15.8 million in assets. Many people think Noriega will have an excellent opportunity to add money laundering to his list of money-making activities through the Institutional Bank of the Fatherland.

Money that is laundered is money that cannot be taxed by the U.S. government. In an effort to recover some of the money, a law was passed in 1988 that gives the government the right to claim the money from illegal drug sales. The federal government filed suit for $433.5 million in laundered drug money from nine American and foreign banks. Drug agents have found that chasing laundered money hurts the cartel more than any other form of interdiction.

Investing in legitimate businesses is another way that drug money is used. In Colombia the cartel is pumping money into the economy, particularly through construction of luxury apartments, shopping malls, hotels, and condominiums. On the surface this seems to be helping the economy, but it also causes prices to go up and the poor are even worse off than before. Some money is put into public works to help the poor. For example, one of the families in the cartel has built free housing for the poor and sports complexes in the city of Medellin, Colombia. Another has given a great deal of money to the Catholic Church, and a third holds horse auctions to help the poor. They point to their "good works" to justify their illegal activities, crime, and violence. It hardly makes up for the murders of judges, policemen, and even cabinet ministers, to say nothing of the people who interfere with their "business" from Colombia throughout Central America and the Caribbean to the U.S.

Not all of the laundered drug money finds its way back to Colombia. In three counties in south Florida it was estimated that one fourth of all real estate investments were made by drug traffickers. Because they have so much money, they can pay premium prices. Consequently, real estate prices have risen considerably. It has created unfair competition for ordinary investors.

Jamaican gangs that supply most of the crack cocaine to the U.S. are based in New York and Florida. They own legitimate businesses and use them in distributing crack.

Drug trafficking is big business all over the world. The cartels are not satisfied with minding their own business; they want to get into legitimate business, too. They corrupt governments, businesses, and individuals. They gain political power through payoffs or fear. Their corruption filters down to affect us all, whether through direct contact with the drugs or a user or being a victim of the crime they bring. You may be in an area that is paying higher real estate prices, and everyone is a victim of higher taxes to pay the cost of fighting their corruption.

SCHOOLS

Drug-prevention programs have become standard in schools throughout the country. The most effective programs begin with kindergarten and continue through high school. The main focus is to keep young people from becoming harmfully involved with drugs. Throughout the country school administrators, teachers, and parents said, "Not our school. Not our kids." Drugs use had become epidemic before adults realized what was going on.

Schools are affected in a variety of ways by drug-abusing students. Drug users don't specialize in cooperation. A degree of rebellion in all teenagers is part of the maturing process. That natural rebellion is magnified when teens get involved with drugs. A few drug-using students can create chaos in a classroom. The disruption caused by a few defiant students interferes with everyone's learning. Students who want to learn and are interested in being successful in school are deprived of the attention they deserve because teachers have to hassle with the troublemakers.

School violence is often started by drug users. They are very easily enraged because they carry around a load of anger all the time. When they're high, they're fearless and will fight anyone. When they're coming down off a high and need a fix, they are often even more dangerous. Most of the time they are time bombs ready to go off at any moment. They are not fun to deal with whether you're an adult at school or a student.

Vandalism in schools has become a major problem in some areas. When teens are high they think it's fun to break things, mess up cafeteria kitchens, destroy science labs, cut down young trees and bushes, spray paint obscenities on walls, grind tires into lawns, and generally ruin anything they can. Local taxpayers bear the expense for all of those things, and students are sickened by the senseless destruction.

Not satisfied with destroying property, users like to bring other people down with them. Introducing others to drugs is high on their lists of fun things to do. They recruit from among other students at school. They make drugs really easy to get. They willingly share with you. They use people as well as drugs.

Most students make their connection for drugs at school. School offers a ready clientele and easy access. School officials are aware of this, and in some areas it isn't so easy to deal on the school grounds. But if that isn't safe they'll be right outside the gates waiting. Teens go to the elementary schools to deal to the younger children. They find a secluded or sheltered place to wait for the younger ones away from the prying eyes of adults. Since being a "narc" is such a taboo, they don't worry too much about the little kids telling on them. The younger ones are easily intimidated, so the drug trade flourishes at school.

Because of the availability of drugs and the exposure to users, schools need drug-prevention programs, and they need them in the early grades. In-servicing school staff is costly and time-consuming, yet necessary. Educating staff to identify users and students who are "at risk" is another important aspect of prevention. Drug education is common in science and health classes. Some states require a course in drug education for graduation. As a result of drug abuse, schools have added a new subject to the curriculum.

Another cost schools pay for the drug abuse of students is a rise in stress of teachers. The pressure of having disruptive, uncooperative students in classes is showing up in absenteeism. Teachers are stressed out and get sick. Many teachers are leaving the profession because they no longer want to deal with the stress. Unfortunately, it is often good teachers who become frustrated when they can't teach because of the constant interruption and interference from troublemakers.

The dropout rate nationally is about 40 percent. Young people who are heavy users generally drop out around eighth grade. Unemployment is high among teens. Those who drop out and want to work have no skills or education, so no one will hire them. If they do get jobs, they're extremely irresponsible and don't hold them for long. Young people on the streets is a national problem. Most resort to stealin' and dealin' or some other form of crime. Girls can usually make a trade for drugs, but many turn to outright prostitution.

Many dropouts leave home and drop out of sight. They become victims of crime themselves. No one knows where they are. They go to other cities and change their names. There's no way to trace them. Some simply disappear and are never heard of again. Drugs rob them of their tomorrows as well as their todays.

Another result of early drug use and dropping out of school is the loss of economic opportunity. Without motivation or a sense of responsibility, people who drop out of school because of drugs seldom if ever get on their feet financially. They're always poor. They often have children when they are very young and don't know how to care for them. They go on welfare and never get off. Society pays the consequences for their use not only because they need assistance but also because they never help share the load. They're always takers and never put anything back. They become the "permanent poor."

Every year since 1975 the National Institute on Drug Abuse (NIDA) has made a survey of high school seniors. Keeping in mind that most heavy drug users never get to be seniors in high school because they drop out, the following are some of the statistics for 1988. The first substantial decrease in cocaine use was reported among high school seniors, and use of other illicit drugs also decreased. Even so, 42 percent reported that during the last year they used some illicit drug, and 57 percent said they had used an illegal drug at least once. Almost a fifth of the seniors (18.7 percent) said they were daily cigarette smokers in 1987. In 1988 daily use of cigarettes dropped to 11 percent, the first significant drop since 1976. The use of all illegal drugs has declined since the peak in the late 1970s and early 1980s, but the legal drug alcohol is still the drug of choice of America's seniors and other teens as well. The percentage of seniors who have had experience with alcohol has stayed at over 90 percent since 1975. Two thirds of the seniors admitted using alcohol in the month before the survey.

The National School Health Survey that was conducted in the fall of 1987 showed that 77 percent of eighth-graders had tried alcohol, and 55 percent of those had tried it by sixth grade. Thirty-four percent of the eighth-graders said they'd had alcohol in the month before the survey, and 26 percent said they'd had five or more drinks on the same occasion during the two weeks before the survey.

Schools constantly have to deal with the tragedy of the death of students because of drunk driving. Some schools have set up crisis centers and have counselors available so students can talk through their grief and deal with the loss of their friends. Drugs, illegal and legal, are having a definite negative impact on our schools.

SPORTS

The consequences of alcohol and cocaine use by well-known sports figures have been talked about for a long time. More recently attention has come to another drug. Although steroids have been used by body-builders and football players for years, it was Ben Johnson's dramatic, crushing fall from the peak of the Olympic mountain in the 1988 Summer Olympic Games in Seoul, Korea, that brought the world's attention to anabolic steroids.

Johnson took steroids to give him that extra burst of

energy, the extra strength in the muscles, that little edge that made him just that much faster than Carl Lewis. His trainer and doctor thought that they'd given him the right kind and the right amount at the right time so that the drug wouldn't show up in his urine. Their miscalculation cost Johnson his dignity and self-respect, to say nothing of humiliation in front of the world. He is lucky it didn't cost him more.

Body-builders and weight-lifters use steroids to build muscles. They appear to be in perfect physical condition. If you could look inside that muscular shell, however, you might see a damaged heart, arteries filled with cholesterol, shrunken testicles, high blood pressure, tumors of the liver and prostate, and severe acne scarring on the chest, back, and shoulders.

After years of daily steroid use, at the height of his career as a weightlifter, billed as the strongest man in the world because he could lift 705 pounds, Glen Maur had a heart attack in 1983. The doctor told him that he had five arteries with 90 to 95 percent blockage and would be dead in three to six months without by-pass surgery. Mauer had a quintuple by-pass operation and knows that his life has been dramatically shortened by his use of steroids.

In West Palm Beach, Florida, Horace Williams was tried, found guilty of murder, and sentenced to life in prison without possibility of parole for twenty-five years. Williams was only twenty-one in September, 1986, when he savagely beat to death a man completely unknown to him in a fit of "roid rage," a common side effect of taking anabolic steroids.

When too much testosterone builds up in the body, it creates a blind, inexplicable rage that goes beyond anger. Some steroid users constantly feel enraged and may strike out at anyone or anything in their way. The frightening thing is that the rage is always present, and no one can tell when it will be triggered. A doctor who works in professional sports believes that the increase in fights and extreme aggression seen in professional sports today is a result of anabolic steroids. The latest rage in sports may be steroids—in more ways than one.

Steroids are being used by young men of high school age

too. Since taking steroids without a prescription is illegal, most of the steroids used by young men are bought illegally on the black market. Without the careful supervision of a doctor, they are even more dangerous. Young men think only of the bulk they'll put on. Cholesterol, tumors, and heart attacks seem a long way away. Acne on back, chest, and shoulders isn't so unusual in teenagers anyway, so who cares? If he's your friend, care enough to talk to him about the dangers of anabolic steroids.

HEALTH

The public health of America is threatened by drugs. The threat used to be hepatitis spread through the use of shared needles and venereal disease and other sexually transmitted diseases that could be cured or, at least, arrested. Today it's AIDS. Intravenous (IV) drug users who are careless about sharing needles spread AIDS, and sexually active people who aren't choosy about their partners and don't use condoms or take care to protect themselves spread AIDS.

Homosexual and bisexual men are most at risk for AIDS. The IV drug users are the second largest at-risk group. Twenty-six percent of all people with AIDS are IV drug users; 19 percent are heterosexual IV drug users, and 7 percent are homosexual or bisexual men who are IV drug users. As of July, 1988, 17,701 of the 68,220 diagnosed cases of AIDS involve IV drug use. That number is expected to double every fourteen to sixteen months. At least one case of an IV drug user with AIDS has been reported in all of the fifty states.

Since about half of the female IV drug users, and some male IV drug users as well, resort to prostitution to support their drug habit, they're at high risk for contracting AIDS and then spreading it to the nonusing population.

Besides the money spent on AIDS research, much is being done to reach the IV drug user. The NIDA has a program that includes seeking out people at risk, educating them about how to reduce risk, encouraging behavior change, and making follow-up contacts to reinforce the change. The

NIDA program is aimed at IV users and their sexual partners.

To be safe, educate yourself on AIDS prevention. It may seem unnecessary to you, but it is a grave public health concern, and you are part of the public.

ALCOHOL

The number one drug of choice among American teenagers is also the drug of choice of the world. Alcohol has been around since ancient times in Africa, Asia, and Europe. It was brought to the Americas and the ocean areas by the Europeans. Its popularity hasn't diminished over the centuries.

When a youth comes home drunk, it's not unusual for parents to say, "Thank God it's not drugs." Alcohol use is so accepted by society that people don't see it as the dangerous drug it is.

In 1987, 23,630 people were killed in alcohol-related automobile accidents. Believe it or not, that's a 17 percent reduction from 1982. For adolescents, the rate has gone down 34 percent. The National Highway Traffic Safety Administration believes that the raising of the drinking age in some states and public education account for the reduction. That still means several thousand young people killed on our highways every year as a result of drunk driving. According to the National Safety Board, about half of all traffic fatalities involve alcohol.

Surgeon General C. Everett Koop wants to see health warning labels on all alcoholic beverages and wants beer and liquor companies to stop using celebrities who appeal to young people in alcoholic beverage advertising.

Drug-prevention programs stress the dangers of illicit drug use while the alcohol use rate of young people stays steadily high. More emphasis must be put on alcohol, the socially acceptable drug. When someone gets drunk and behaves stupidly, people brush it off with, "Oh, ya know, he was drunk." Friends laugh and joke about what happened when someone was drunk. Until people become obnoxious and do something outrageous, everyone excuses their behavior because they were drunk and just having a good time.

Besides death on the roads, crimes of violence are connected with alcohol. Often domestic violence occurs when someone has been drinking. Shootings and stabbings and fights in general are more likely to happen when people are drunk.

Professor J. Westermeyer of the University of Minnesota reported in his paper "Cultural patterns of drug and alcohol use, an analysis of host and agent in the cultural environment" that "U.S. citizens of Irish origin have a high rate of arrests involving inebriety." Persons of European ancestry have a high rate of suicide associated with alcohol use, and African-Americans and American Indians have a high rate of homicide associated with alcohol use.

Societies around the world are beginning to realize the destruction that alcohol abuse can bring. In recent years the Soviet government has tried to control the consumption of vodka in the USSR. They tried to limit the amount that people could buy; they tried penalties. Nothing worked. Experts in alcoholism treatment from the U.S. were consulted, and a contract was made with a U.S. treatment provider to work with a Soviet team to develop a treatment program for their country.

In 1988 a report of prevention programs in twenty-nine countries was developed through help from the World Health Organization. Finland, Ireland, and Poland reported alcohol as a major problem. In addition, Canada, France, and the United Kingdom see alcohol as a much bigger problem than other drug use. Even with the availability of coca paste, the favorite form of cocaine in Peru, alcohol looms as the greater drug problem. In recent years coca paste has been catching up, but alcohol still hangs in there in as the Peruvian leader.

The abuse of alcohol is a major problem throughout the world. It is important to remember that alcohol is a mood-altering drug and is just as dangerous and destructive as other psychoactive drugs. In the National School Health Survey, 80 percent of students believed there is a moderate or great risk from *regular* use of alcohol; 80 percent of the same students see a moderate or great risk from *occasional* use of marijuana, and 88 percent think there is moderate or great risk from *occasional* use of cocaine. The drug they know is perceived to be less risky, when, in fact, alcohol deserves the same respect given to any other powerful drug.

SUBSTANCE ABUSE AND YOU

What does all this mean in *your* life? All the time you were ignoring the news about Noriega, you had no idea that the murder reported in the streets of a city in your state might have been over a drug deal made possible by the drug corridor in Panama. Although you never knew that gangs from Jamaica are the chief crack suppliers, your grandmother's house was burglarized by a crack user who needed money for his drug. You have nothing to do with that scuzzy druggie down the street, but he's offering marijuana to the kid next door.

The two wise-mouths who hassle your third period teacher are cheating you out of your education. Your family may not be going on much of a vacation this year because your parents' taxes were more than they expected. You're helping to pay for the drug war.

Remember what a neat guy Jeff used to be, and how Sherry used to be so much fun? Now they're hanging around the party crowd getting drunk and stoned. It's too bad, because they used to be good kids.

It was hard to take when four kids from your school were wiped out in one accident after the Senior Prom. Too bad someone didn't take the keys away from Greg. Maybe you should get involved with the group planning a sober graduation.

Mark sure thinks he's rough and tough since he started lifting weights. He may have a great body, but that doesn't give him any right to be rude to people. He used to be a nice guy, but now it's as though he has a chip on his shoulder. Nobody wants to be around him because he gets mad over nothing. Do you suppose he got help with those muscles from steroids? He may be showing the first signs of "roid rage."

You may be "squeaky clean," but you can't avoid the effects of drug abuse. They're all around you. You may think you can't do anything about it, but you can. Groups all over the nation are promoting a drug-free life-style. Community agencies have programs for older teens to join that provide drug-prevention education for younger children. If your school doesn't have a SADD (Students Against Driving Drunk) group, talk to a teacher or counselor who might be interested in helping you start one. Talk to your friends. Check out what's going on in your community and get involved. You may think that one person can't make a difference. When people work together, a difference *can* be made. Doing nothing changes nothing. Be a part of positive change.

Appendix

RESOURCE LIST

Telephone Book

Yellow pages—Alcoholism, Drug Abuse, Counselors
White pages—Alcoholics Anonymous, Al-Anon, Narcotics
Anonymous, National Council on Alcoholism, Alcoholism Counseling, Drug Abuse Services
Government listings—Alcoholism Treatment, Drug Abuse,
County Health Services

A.A World Services, Inc.
P.O. Box 459
Grand Central Station
New York, NY 10163

Al-Anon Family Group Headquarters
P.O. Box 182
Madison Square Station
New York, NY 10159

Narcotics Anonymous
World Service Office
16155 Wyandotte Street
Van Nuys, CA 91406

National Council on Alcoholism
12 West 21st Street
New York, NY 10010

National Association of Children of Alcoholics
31706 Coast Highway
South Laguna, CA 92677

Index